YORK NOTES

General Editors: Professor A.N.Jeffares (*University of Stirling*) & Professor Suheil Bushrui (*American University of Beirut*)

Charles Dickens

TIMES

Notes by Dominic Hyland

MA (CAMBRIDGE) M ED (MANCHESTER)

LONGMAN
YORK PRESS

YORK PRESS
Immeuble Esseily, Place Riad Solh, Beirut.

LONGMAN GROUP UK LIMITED
Longman House, Burnt Mill, Harlow,
Essex CM20 2JE, England
Associated companies, branches and representatives
throughout the world

First published 1981
Ninth impression 1992

ISBN 0-582-79215-0

Printed in Hong Kong
WC/09

Contents

Part 1

Introduction

The life of Charles Dickens

Charles Dickens was born on 7 February 1812 at Portsea, near Portsmouth. His father was John Dickens who was at that time a clerk in the Naval Pay Office in Portsmouth Dockyard. In March, Charles was christened in the parish church, St Mary's in Kingston, and given the names Charles John Huffam. In June of the same year, the family moved to another address in Portsea. Exactly two years later they moved again; this time it was to London where John Dickens had a job in Somerset House. The family now lived in Norfolk Street, St Pancras.

This constant moving was to become familiar to Dickens. By the time he was five they were living at Chatham in Kent. Dickens's father was always in debt, and it was as the result of his carelessness with money that they were forced to move again, when Charles was nine, to 18 St Mary's Place, Chatham. They moved again the following year to Camden Town in London. Within the year they moved yet again to Gower Street, London. In 1824, John Dickens was arrested for debt and sent to the Marshalsea debtors' prison. The rest of the family joined him there, but Charles himself was spared this humiliation and was lodged instead with a Mrs Poylance in Camden Town. In the same year, 1824, he gained his first employment—at Warren's blacking factory where he received six shillings a week for sealing and labelling pots of blacking.

In May 1824, John Dickens was released from the Marshalsea and Charles was able to leave his work, though it did seem to be his mother's wish that he stay on at the blacking warehouse! He went to school at Wellington House Academy, Hampstead Road. The following year, the Dickens family moved to Somers Town. Two years later they were evicted for not paying their rates. This coincided with Dickens's joining the firm of Ellis and Blackmore at 5 Holborn Court, Gray's Inn, as a solicitor's clerk.

His father and he can be said to have joined careers in the years immediately following, for they both learned shorthand and John became a reporter with the *Morning Herald* while Charles worked as a freelance reporter in the Courts. In 1831, Charles worked for his uncle John Henry Barrow, reporting for the *Mirror of Parliament*, and the following year for an evening paper called *The True Sun*. Charles was now twenty and courting a girl called Maria Beadnell. The family was still not settled, having moved again three times in as many years. Dickens's relationship with Maria was not to be a lasting one: they parted in 1833, a year before Dickens met the woman who was to be his wife, Catherine Hogarth. This happened when the Dickens family was living at 18 Bentinck Street, an address they had to leave in 1834 because John Dickens was yet again arrested for debt.

On 2 April 1836, Charles married Catherine Hogarth, who was to bear him thirteen children. This marriage lasted effectively until May 1858 when the two separated. Dickens was then involved with the actress Ellen Ternan whom he met in August 1857. In that year, he completed *Little Dorrit*, the novel that succeeded *Hard Times* which he had written in 1854. After the breakdown of his marriage, Dickens completed only three more major novels: *A Tale of Two Cities*, *Great Expectations*, and *Our Mutual Friend*. But over the twelve years that elapsed until his death in 1870 he was in no way idle. There was still a steady outpouring of stories, much travelling about Britain and America, giving readings from his novels, and starting a new weekly journal which he called *All The Year Round*. This was an appropriate title, in that it aptly described the ceaseless labours of the man who founded the journal. By the time of his death, Dickens had written fifteen novels in addition to many humorous sketches and stories and his five Christmas books, as well as work for operas and dramatic productions.

Historical background

Dickens was born during the Regency, a period famous for the elegance of the Prince Regent's court. Yet in the year of Dickens's birth there were riots in England, carried out by a group called the Luddites who opposed the introduction of factory machinery and the advance of industrialisation. They were unemployed men who thought that their troubles were mainly caused by the arrival of the machines which for them represented the Industrial Revolution. Much of this part of the century was disturbed by similar unrest. In 1819, for example, people protesting in Manchester against the crippling Corn Laws were run down by cavalry in St Peter's Field. Though only eleven people were killed this incident came to be known as the Peterloo Massacre. The two themes of machines against men and of hungry workers recur in a number of key scenes in Dickens's *Hard Times*. Not least among these is Bounderby's interview with Stephen Blackpool. There, Dickens tells us that Stephen goes to see Bounderby at his home where he is having his 'chop and sherry' lunch. Obviously, Bounderby eats well. We are to presume that the lot of his workers is less attractive. In order to emphasise this, Dickens has Bounderby suggest that the workers' demands are extreme:

> You don't expect to be set up in a coach and six, and to be fed on turtle soup and venison, with a gold spoon, as a good many of 'em do! (p.109)

The workers of the time had no formal associations or trade unions. Various efforts were made to form such organisations, but these were inevitably frustrated and met by force. In 1834, for example, there occurred the notorious case of the Tolpuddle martyrs. A group of agricultural workers in Tolpuddle, Dorset, made an effort to form such a union, and were transported to Australia for their actions. Two years later, as a result of public protest, a pardon was offered to them.

Such public protests were a feature of the time, and Dickens describes one in the famous trade union scene with Slackbridge in *Hard Times*. An important form of public protest was the rise of the People's Charter in 1838 which made mainly political demands. This was a large movement and caused considerable public disturbance. However, it never achieved its aims for various reasons, two main ones being that Parliament simply ignored the demands of the Chartists, and that the movement was ineffectually organised. By 1854, when *Hard Times* appeared, Chartism no longer had any political significance.

To gain first-hand knowledge of union activities amongst the cotton workers of Preston ('Coketown' of *Hard Times*) Dickens travelled to that Lancashire town. There had been a strike there which had lasted several weeks. Here is a ballad that was circulating at that time describing that event:

The Cotton Lords of Preston

Have you not heard the news of late
About some mighty men so great?
I mean the swells of Fishergate,
The Cotton Lords of Preston.
They are a set of stingy blades
They've locked up all their mills and shades.
So now we've nothing else to do
But come a-singing songs to you.
So with our ballads we've come out
To tramp the country round about,
And try if we cannot live without
The Cotton Lords of Preston.

Chorus:
Everybody's crying shame
On these gentlemen by name.
Don't you think they're much to blame,
The Cotton Lords of Preston?

The working people such as we
Pass their time in misery
While they live in luxury,
The Cotton Lords of Preston.
They're making money every way
And building factories every day,
Yet when we ask them for more pay
They had the impudence to say:
'To your demands we'll not consent;
You get enough, so be content'—
But we will have the ten per cent
From the Cotton Lords of Preston.

Our masters say they're very sure
That the strike we can't endure;
They all assert we're very poor,
The Cotton Lords of Preston;
But we've determined every one
With them we will not be done,
And we will not be content
Until we get the ten per cent.
The Cotton Lords are sure to fall,
Both ugly, handsome, short or tall;
For we intent to conquer all
The Cotton Lords of Preston.

So men and women, all of you,
Come and buy a song or two,
And assist us to subdue
The Cotton Lords of Preston.
We'll conquer them and no mistake,
Whatever laws they seem to make
And when we get the ten per cent
Then we'll live happy and content.

Bounderby in *Hard Times* is obviously typical of the Cotton Lords.
They were supported in Parliament by men whom Dickens satirises in
Hard Times as the Hard Facts men. Thomas Gradgrind was one such
Parliamentarian, representing the party of 'Hard Facts'. The econ-
omic thinking behind this party was that of *laissez-faire* ('do as

you please') which argued for free enterprise without government interference. The notion of *laissez faire* originated in the work of Adam Smith (1723–90), notably in his book *The Wealth of Nations* (1776). Notice that one of Thomas Gradgrind's children is called Adam Smith.

However attractive the notion of free enterprise may appear in principle, its results as depicted by Dickens's characters—Bounderby perhaps in particular—are less desirable. Bounderby's interests are entirely selfish. There is little evidence in him of what Jeremy Bentham (1748–1832), the eighteenth-century philosopher, described as 'the greatest good for the greatest number', an axiom often quoted in support of the principle of *laissez faire*. No study of the historical background of *Hard Times* would be complete without a mention of Thomas Carlyle (1795–1881) to whom the novel is dedicated. He was a severe critic of political and economic developments in the nineteenth century. Here, for example, is a statement from his *Signs of the Times* written in 1829 which can be easily seen as a precursor to many of Dickens's own statements in *Hard Times*:

> Were we required to characterise this age of ours by any single epithet, we should be tempted to call it not an Heroical, Devotional, Philosophical, or Moral Age, but, above all others, the Mechanical Age. It is the Age of Machinery in every outward and inward sense of that word; the age which, with its whole undivided might, forwards, teaches and practises the great art of adapting means to ends. Nothing is now done directly or by hand; all is by rule and calculated contrivance .... Men are grown mechanical in head and in heart, as well as in hand.

Notice here Carlyle's concern with the term 'hand' and his regret that so little human or humane contact is still in evidence, and that all has been given over to machines. This is something that Dickens remarks on throughout his novel—the irony of the term 'Hands' in his book used to describe the workers is obviously something that fascinates him. Dickens insists that the important thing to value and preserve is the sacredness of the individual—that 'unfathomable mystery'—which contrasts so vividly with the insensibility of the machine:

> So many hundred Hands in this Mill; so many hundred horse Steam Power. It is known, to the force of a single pound weight, what the engine will do; but, not all the calculators of the National Debt can tell me the capacity for good or evil, for love or hatred, for patriotism or discontent, for the decomposition of virtue into vice, or the reverse, at any single moment in the soul of one of these its quiet servants, with the composed faces and the regulated actions. (p.108)

The work of Charles Dickens

When Dickens died on 9 June 1870 at the age of fifty-eight he had produced a prodigious number of works. These included his fifteen novels as well as a variety of other writings. His industry is evident in the speed with which his various works were produced. In the four years from 1838 to 1841, for example, he wrote four major novels: *Oliver Twist*, *Nicholas Nickleby*, *The Old Curiosity Shop* and *Barnaby Rudge*. In addition to his writing Dickens toured in America—his first visit was in 1842—and this gave rise to the entertaining *American Notes*. He was also involved in editing newspapers, founding journals (*Household Words* and *All The Year Round*), writing, producing and acting in plays, and giving innumerable successful public readings of his works.

Dickens's novels were initially serialised in either monthly or weekly parts. Serialisation was a common practice in the nineteenth century. It was a technique used by publishers to increase sales. Dickens used it himself, and with *Hard Times* boosted the sale of his journal *Household Words* whose existence was threatened at the time. Nine of his fifteen novels originally appeared in monthly parts, each containing three or four chapters. Five, including *Hard Times* were serialised, under pressure, in weekly parts. Although there was plenty of evidence of the vigour of his ready invention in his novels, while writing *Hard Times* Dickens complained to his great friend and biographer John Forster (1812–76) that 'the spring does not seem to fly back again directly as it always did when I put my own work aside and had nothing else to do'. Dickens is here using a mechanical metaphor to describe his own work!

Dickens's stories were immensely popular, but even at the height of his popularity he was subject to failure. One such relative failure led to a clash with his publishers, Chapman and Hall. The sales of *Martin Chuzzlewit* (1843–4) were below their expectations, and, indeed, below those of Dickens himself who had thought of it as one of his greatest novels. Chapman and Hall had a contract with Dickens which stipulated that the author would receive less if the sales of his novels did not produce acceptable levels of profit. They enforced this contract and Dickens then changed his publishers to Bradbury and Evans, who published *Hard Times*.

A note on the text

The Penguin English Library Edition of *Hard Times* is the edition quoted in these Notes. The text used there is that of the first volume edition, published by Bradbury & Evans, London, in 1854.

Hard Times had already appeared in weekly parts in Dickens's periodical *Household Words*. The first episode appeared in No. 210 in April 1854, the last in August of the same year in issue No. 229. The major difference between those weekly parts and the edition published by Bradbury and Evans was that in the latter Dickens added titles to his chapters and to the three books into which the novel is divided: Sowing, Reaping and Garnering.

Part 2

Summaries
of HARD TIMES

A general summary

The sub-titles to the three parts of the novel—Sowing, Reaping, and Garnering—call to mind the biblical words 'As ye sow, so also shall ye reap'. These words would have been familiar to Victorian readers, and could be found framed and enshrined and displayed in many a middle-class Victorian home. They had a special reference to the upbringing and education of children. They suggested that the grounding children received in their formative years would directly affect their adult lives. The seeds that were sowed in childhood would bear fruit in later years. If early influences were good and wholesome the results would meet with approval and acceptance by society. If the early influences were bad then the outcome would be disastrous. Dickens uses this notion in the opening chapter of *Hard Times* in the educational environment he provides in the classroom. There he openly suggests two forms of educational emphasis. One is on the place of facts, the other is on the place of the imagination. These conflicting emphases are presented in various guises throughout the novel. At the same time, the irony of the agricultural metaphor of sowing and reaping gains considerable significance, given the novel's preoccupation with industrialism.

The novel opens in the classroom, and there Thomas Gradgrind is introduced addressing the class in what is called his 'model school'. He is insisting on the value of facts and the dangers of the imagination. It is ironic that immediately after this he finds his two eldest children, Tom and Louisa, seeking the very thing he was denouncing: the expression of the imagination. They are peeping into a circus ring. Further irony is added by the fact that Gradgrind had earlier rebuked a child called Sissy Jupe whose father works at the circus. It would at this point be more accurate to say that Sissy's father had worked at the circus, for he has recently abandoned it and his daughter.

It had been Gradgrind's intention to advise Mr Jupe (or, as he is known at the circus, Signor Jupe) that his daughter could no longer attend the school. Instead, despite the harsh impression we have of Gradgrind at this stage of the novel, he agrees to accept the now orphaned Sissy into his own household as a companion to his daughter Louisa. He is warned of the ill consequences of this action by his friend Josiah Bounderby—a rich industrialist who, we learn, has always been inordinately fond of Louisa. Indeed, he marries her early in the novel. Louisa, on her part, agrees to the marriage simply to please her brother, Tom, who is looking for a position in Bounderby's bank. Louisa is eighteen and Bounderby fifty when they marry.

Shortly before his marriage to Louisa, Bounderby agrees to an interview with a worker at his mill named Stephen Blackpool, who is much troubled by his unhappy marriage. He has been married for nineteen years but the marriage has not been a success. His wife is an alcoholic and has been unfaithful to him. He asks Bounderby for advice how to gain release from his wife. Bounderby and his housekeeper, Mrs Sparsit, are appalled by the suggestion of divorce and can offer Stephen no help or consolation. He is in love with another woman called Rachael and is anxious to marry her.

Soon after this we meet Rachael. She is nursing Stephen's sick wife who has returned unannounced to Stephen's impoverished lodgings. On his way back to these lodgings Stephen had met an old woman who, we later find, is called Mrs Pegler, and is Bounderby's much abused mother. After Bounderby's marriage Mrs Sparsit takes up residence over Bounderby's bank whilst Louisa and Bounderby take a house in the country. There they are visited by James Harthouse, an idle gentleman of good family who is vaguely interested in 'going in' for politics.

The major character list is now complete. The story rapidly changes from a study of industrial life—though there is a vital section dealing with industrial relations—into a kind of detective story. For Tom robs the bank and puts the blame on the unfortunate Stephen Blackpool. As luck would have it, the robbery coincides with Stephen's departure from Coketown after he had been rejected by his work-mates for disobeying trade union rules. This strand of the plot runs parallel with another, dealing with the apparently illicit relationship between Louisa and James Harthouse. Both these associations prove equally ill-founded. Stephen is exonerated from the robbery charge in a melodramatic episode and the chase turns into the pursuit of the real criminal, Tom. Louisa, for her part, flees from Harthouse in a storm and seeks and finds a reconciliation with her father.

Detailed summaries

BOOK THE FIRST: *SOWING*

Chapter 1: The One Thing Needful

The novel opens with the booming voice of Mr Gradgrind filling a large classroom with his sentiments about Facts and the need for a pragmatic view of the world. He sees this as the essence of a sound education. At this stage, he is unidentified by name, but carefully described physically as being of a threatening and unattractive appearance. He is in the company of two other adults, one the schoolmaster, the other totally anonymous.

COMMENTARY: Dickens's chapter heading is taken from the story of Martha and Mary in the Gospels. These are two sisters whom Jesus befriends. When Jesus visits them Martha busies herself while Mary sits and listens quietly to Jesus. Martha complains that Mary is doing nothing, but Jesus replies that Mary has chosen 'the one thing ... needful' (Luke 10: 42).

The irony, then, in Dickens's chapter heading would not be lost on Victorian readers who were well versed in the Scriptures. Jesus is making an appeal for a quiet, almost passive life, one free of the pursuit of material things. Gradgrind, on the other hand, is inculcating the need for 'nothing but Facts'. Dickens sets the scene economically: its tone will thus influence the whole novel. Here is a confrontation between an adult world that is uncomfortably aggressive and acquisitive and the submissive and even cowering world of children, the 'little vessels then and there arranged in order, ready to have imperial gallons of facts poured into them'.

Dickens devotes a paragraph to a description, in typically exaggerated manner, of the unimaginative make-up of his speaker. The word 'square' is used five times and is echoed by the emphasis on straight lines and dark recesses. There is a repetitiveness in the style which echoes, too, the insistent repetition of the speaker's bald view of life—notice, for example, the reiteration of the phrase 'The emphasis was helped' in the opening of four consecutive sentences. Notice, too, the ironic intrusion of Dickens's own inventiveness in the imagery which contrasts sharply with the speaker's attack on imagination:

The emphasis was helped by the speaker's hair, which bristled on the skirts of his bald head, a plantation of firs to keep the wind from its shining surface, all covered with knobs, like the crust of a plum pie.

NOTES AND GLOSSARY:

commodious cellarage: a description of the eye-sockets as resembling rather deep cellars
skirts of his bald head: his bald head was fringed with hair
obstinate carriage: the way he stood made him appear stubborn and unmoving
little vessels: Dickens compares the heads of the young children to empty containers which are to be filled
imperial gallons: the standard measure of liquids (4.54 litres)

Chapter 2: Murdering the Innocents

At this point, the speaker is introduced by name as Thomas Gradgrind, and is now described in greater detail. He addresses one of the pupils, identifying her by her number in the class, not by her name. She introduces herself as Sissy Jupe. He takes offence at this version of her given name and insists that she is properly called Cecilia. When she points out that her father calls her Sissy he takes the opportunity of questioning her about her father. He, it appears, works with horses in a circus. Gradgrind then insists on hearing a definition of a horse, and when Sissy fails to produce it, he turns his attention to another pupil called Bitzer who promptly delivers a dictionary definition of a horse.

At this point, one of the other adults in the room—obviously an inspector of schools—asks his own question of the class in general. He asks whether they would paper a room in their house with pictures of horses. The children's first response is in the affirmative. His obvious disapproval persuades them to change this to a negative! The only dissenters are a fat boy and Sissy Jupe. The first is soon dealt with, but Sissy proves much less amenable. She puts the case for the play of imagination but is promptly shouted down by the government inspector. He then yields place to the third adult present who is apparently a probationer teacher, called M'Choakunchild. Dickens describes the type of training this teacher had received and suggests that it was really inappropriate to what should have been his goals in education.

COMMENTARY: The chapter title again has biblical origins. It is taken from the New Testament and refers to the slaughter of all male infants at the time of the birth of Christ. Thus Dickens's title has a rather grim humour to it. His depiction of the two leading 'innocents', Sissy and Bitzer, is achieved by means of contrasts. Sissy is described as dark and obviously full of promise; Bitzer, on his part, is anaemic and colourless, an obvious product of the soulless education to which he has been subjected. His definition of a horse demonstrates how far he is removed from real life; indeed he is shown to be at the other end, literally, of the light spectrum: 'Sissy . . . came in for the beginning of a sunbeam, of which Bitzer . . . caught the end.' Dickens sees this as typical of Bitzer, so much so that he refers to it again when we meet this character afresh in Chapter One of the Second Book:

> He was a very light porter indeed; as light as in the days when he blinkingly defined a horse, for girl number twenty.

This is a useful instance of Dickens's compact composition in this novel. He is often accused of a lack of continuity in his work, but in Hard Times he seems very concerned with a sense of unity of structure.

This chapter does much to reinforce the message of the 'facts' school: that one ought to look for reality and not for the fruits of the imagination. This is the motive behind the protracted episode relating to room decoration with which the chapter concludes. Dickens's tendency to exaggeration and repetition is well illustrated here, and its rather crude intrusiveness is highlighted in his choice of name for the new teacher beginning his career in the blind perpetuation of facts.

NOTES AND GLOSSARY:

a rule: a ruler used for measurement

little pitchers: another reference to the 'vessels' in Chapter One waiting to be filled with facts

a galvanizing apparatus: Dickens's image here is borrowed from Mary Shelley's (1797–1851) Gothic story *Frankenstein* (1818). Frankenstein created his own monster by the use of electricity

girl number twenty: in large classrooms of the time, there were so many pupils that they were given numbers for ease of reference

quadruped: having four feet

Chapter 3: A Loophole

Thomas Gradgrind makes his way home to Stone Lodge and Dickens once more enlarges on the need, as Gradgrind sees it, for a factual approach to life. We learn that there are five children in the Gradgrind household. They have all been reared on the principle of Fact and the avoidance of wonder. They had never, for example, heard any nursery rhymes or fairy stories. With this as a background, it is easy to imagine Gradgrind's annoyance when on his way home he finds two of his children, Louisa and Tom, stealing a peep at the circus which has come to town and in which Sissy Jupe's father is a star performer. When confronted by her father Louisa defends herself bravely and expresses her disillusionment with her life. She is, as Dickens tells us, 'fifteen or sixteen'. Gradgrind insists that the two children should go home with him and, as they walk along, his total concern appears to be what Mr Bounderby would think of them if he ever discovered their misdeed.

COMMENTARY: Dickens establishes certain themes in his story very economically here: one is the sense of rebellion in the Gradgrind children; another is Tom's reliance on Louisa, which will be of central importance in the novel; a third is the importance of Bounderby as one whose influence will dominate the novel.

Already we are becoming aware of the construction and composition of the novel. The links are being established between the three households: the Jupes, the Gradgrinds and the Bounderbys. This linking of families is to be one of the main elements in the plot of the novel. Dickens took great pains over such details. In a letter to a friend he wrote: 'I am in a dreary state planning and planning the story of *Hard Times*.' With the introduction of Merrylegs and Signor Jupe, Dickens offers a taste of the humour of which he is capable but which is largely absent here. There is irony, there is exaggeration, but there is very little light humour in this novel.

NOTES AND GLOSSARY:

a face in the moon: a reference to the traditional nursery tale of a man who had been banished to the moon for gathering sticks on the Sabbath

Twinkle, twinkle . . . : Dickens gives here the first two lines of a famous nursery rhyme

the Great Bear: a constellation of stars

Professor Owen: Sir Richard Owen (1804–92) who was a physician and comparative anatomist and not a star-gazer as Dickens's humour might suggest

Charles's Wain: another formation of stars

that famous cow: Dickens refers here to another well-known children's nursery rhyme, 'The House that Jack Built'

Tom Thumb: the main character in a fairy story of the same name

conchological: to do with shells

Peter Piper: a reference to another verse for children in the form of a tongue-twister much like Dickens's parody here

suffrages: votes (here, of confidence)

in an ecclesiastical niche of early Gothic architecture: a humorous reference to Sleary's 'box office' which is compared here to a recess in a medieval church where the statue of a saint would be housed

House of Correction: name for a prison where convicts underwent reformatory treatment under very harsh conditions

Mrs Grundy: prudish old lady, much feared by her neighbours, from the play *Speed the Plough*

Chapter 4: Mr Bounderby

The sense of continuity is enhanced here by the immediate link between the conclusion of the preceding chapter and the beginning of this one. Where Gradgrind could be summed up as square, Bounderby, by contrast, is decidedly round like a balloon. He, too, like Gradgrind, is bald, and Dickens relates his baldness to the wind in terms not unlike those used in Chapter One to describe Gradgrind. We first meet him standing in front of the fire at Stone Lodge talking to Mrs Gradgrind of the poverty he experienced in his youth, and how he overcame that poverty to become the successful self-made man he is now. Mrs Gradgrind is seen as totally feeble and submissive, plagued by ill-health. As a mother she is obviously as useless as the mother who, Bounderby claims, abandoned him as a child. When Thomas Gradgrind enters the room with the two culprits, Louisa and Tom, Mrs Gradgrind can only complain that their ill-advised actions have aggravated her headache.

In the conversation which follows Gradgrind and Bounderby establish to their satisfaction that Sissy Jupe's presence in the school has had a bad effect on Tom and Louisa. They agree that she must be forced to leave the school immediately and they set off to inform her father of that fact. Before leaving, Bounderby shows his interest in Louisa by giving her a kiss and calling her 'my pet'.

COMMENTARY: Dickens is adding rapidly to the list of characters in this novel. You should notice that the new characters are typical of the caricatures for which he is famous. Bounderby is described in terms emphasising his roundness and coarseness, and exaggerates everything about himself. Mrs Gradgrind is a lesser figure in both literary and literal terms. It is her feebleness that Dickens chooses as his focal point for her.

Three other Gradgrinds are introduced and Dickens gives two of them names which serve to highlight again the type of thinking that he is satirising in much of the novel: that of Adam Smith and Malthus. The poignancy of the children's plight—and poignancy is an effect Dickens strives to achieve in this novel—is captured in the single scene of Jane, the third child, having fallen asleep over her problem in mathematics. Bounderby's designs on Louisa are broadly hinted at in the concluding scene of this chapter where he forces his attentions on her. Louisa's developing insensitivity, the result of her mechanical education, and her silent dislike of Mr Bounderby, are sharply brought to our notice in her concluding remarks to Tom: 'You may cut the piece out with your penknife if you like, Tom. I wouldn't cry!'

NOTES AND GLOSSARY:

chandler: a dealer in candles and groceries

Adam Smith: a Scottish economist (1723–90) who advocated free trade and *laissez-faire*

Thomas Robert Malthus: English economist and churchman (1766–1834) who advocated population control

Chapter 5: The Key-note

Dickens describes Coketown in all its horror. He makes an attack on the soulless architecture of the place as well as the irrelevance of the spiritual features of the town. He draws an analogy between the soullessness of Coketown and the bleak rationalism of the Gradgrinds.

Gradgrind and Bounderby are searching for Signor Jupe and have been told he lives at Pond's End. They are suddenly halted by the sight of Sissy Jupe pursued by Bitzer who literally bumps into Gradgrind. The latter rebukes him and sends him on his way. Gradgrind then asks Sissy to take them to see her father, to which she readily agrees.

COMMENTARY: The paths of the main characters in the novel are already beginning to cross. Bounderby has now met both Bitzer and Sissy Jupe and thus establishes still further common ground with Gradgrind.

The etching in of the picture of Coketown comes at a relatively late point in the novel. Dickens usually invests his story with plenty of environmental detail earlier than this: we might compare the fog scene which opens *Bleak House* (1852–3)—the novel, incidentally, which immediately preceded *Hard Times*—with his depiction of the 'serpents of smoke' that introduces this chapter.

His virulent attack on formal, organised religion, as well as upon the philanthropic societies represented by the 'Teetotal Society' is a familiar feature of Dickens's novels of social criticism.

In this chapter Dickens strives to add some degree of complexity to his characterisation of Gradgrind, who is here given another dimension: 'His character was not unkind, all things considered; it might have been a very kind one indeed, if he had only made some round mistake in the arithmetic that balanced it, years ago.' Dickens is thus introducing a sense of conflict within the character, which anticipates the moral dilemma which will confront Gradgrind in the course of the novel.

Dickens's treatment of religion is very much in the spirit of Carlyle's description of its mechanical nature in his *Signs of the Times*:

> Then, we have Religious machines, of all imaginable varieties; the Bible society, professing a far higher and heavenly structure, is found, on enquiry, to be an altogether earthly contrivance: supported by collection of moneys, by fomenting of vanities, by puffing, intrigue and chicane; a machine for converting the Heathen.

In this chapter Dickens speaks of the church as a 'pious warehouse' in a town 'sacred to fact'.

NOTES AND GLOSSARY:

Teetotal Society: a reference to the many temperance societies flourishing during this time, whose members refrained from alcoholic drink

Mocha coffee: fine coffee, originally from Mocha, an Arabian port

---

Chapter 6: Sleary's Horsemanship

Sissy takes Gradgrind and Bounderby to the Pegasus's Arms where she and her father live. She expects to find him there together with his dog, Merrylegs. But they are not there, and she leaves Gradgrind and Bounderby in a room at the inn while she goes in search of them. Whilst she is away, a couple of performers from the circus, E.W.B. Childers and a dwarf known as Kidderminster, inform the two men that Sissy's father has left for good, abandoning his daughter. Childers points out that he probably did so, ironically enough, in his daughter's best interests, and he tells Gradgrind and Bounderby that Signor Jupe was particularly concerned that she should have proper schooling.

At this juncture, all the circus folk appear, including their leader, Sleary. He asks the visitors to be kind to Sissy when she comes back. But Bounderby, intent on facts, tells Sissy bluntly that her father has left her. The circus performers are annoyed at his lack of feeling, and Sleary hints that they might throw Bounderby out of the window. Gradgrind saves the day by assuring Sissy that she may stay at the school and live in his house if she so wishes. If she decides to stay with him, though, she must on no account have any more dealings with the circus people. Sleary, on his part, assures Sissy that she would be welcome to stay with them. Sissy has been assured that her father could always find her at Gradgrind's. She collects her belongings, having decided in favour of Gradgrind and education.

COMMENTARY: Decision-making plays an important part in this chapter. Gradgrind and Bounderby have to decide what to do with Sissy as her father has absconded. Gradgrind shows his worth—and thus adds to the effect of being more than a caricature—by speaking out for Sissy and offering her a home and education.

Signor Jupe has already made his decision, and Sissy herself has had to resolve her dilemma quickly and irrevocably. In this chapter, too, Dickens pulls out all the stops in his efforts to achieve a poignant effect. The kindness of the circus people and their obvious affection for Sissy are part of this effect. The speech impediment the author gives to Sleary also helps to make his character more sympathetic while adding to the sense of oddity and eccentricity that Dickens likes to offer as entertainment to his reader.

NOTES AND GLOSSARY:

Pegasus: a winged horse in Greek mythology

a pigtail bolt upright: this describes a comical cap used by Jupe in his circus act

the ark: a reference to Noah's Ark in the Old Testament into which, at the time of the Great Flood, Noah took a pair of each kind of living animal

Centaur: the half-man, half-horse of Greek mythology

carmine: a crimson pigment made from cochineal and applied here to the face to add redness

bismuth: a reddish-white metal

Cupid: the Roman god of love

goosed: hissed and booed by the audience

Dick Jones of Wapping: meaning a person of no importance

Punch: a comic figure in a puppet play

morrithed: that is, 'morrised', meaning 'run away'. The term comes from the morris dance, a quick skipping folk dance (Sleary pronounces 's' as 'th')

Chapter 7: Mrs Sparsit

Dickens introduces yet another character of eccentric appearance, with an odd background. Mrs Sparsit claims to come from a respectable family but has fallen on hard times. She is now housekeeper to Bounderby, who treats her with inordinate respect. Having her as his housekeeper adds of course to the esteem in which he holds himself and in which he expects others to hold him.

Sissy Jupe is at this time staying at Bounderby's before going to Stone Lodge. Bounderby had insisted on this to give Gradgrind time to reflect on his decision to give Sissy a home. Bounderby is unsympathetic to Sissy and concerned that she might in some way contaminate Louisa. Mrs Sparsit tries to ingratiate herself with Bounderby by saying 'You are quite another father to Louisa, sir.' Bounderby insists, however, that he is better seen as a father to Tom Gradgrind, whom he plans to employ at the bank once Tom has finished his education. This conversation with Mrs Sparsit is interrupted by the arrival of Gradgrind and Louisa, who have come to collect Sissy. The three set off for Stone Lodge without exchanging a word.

COMMENTARY: Mrs Sparsit's role in the novel is indicated by her having a chapter dedicated to her, a privilege she shares with only one character in the book so far. It is another sign of Dickens's concern to maintain unity of structure in the novel that Mrs Sparsit's role is so carefully sustained throughout. She does not fade from view but makes her presence felt consistently. There is more than a faint hint of irony in her praise of Bounderby's kindness towards Louisa. Dickens indicates later that Mrs Sparsit expected herself to be made his wife!

Gradgrind's decision to befriend Sissy can be seen as Dickens's way of continuing to win sympathy for the man from his readers. Despite his bluff approach to Sissy, we are assured that his intentions, at least, are pure in contrast to Bounderby's wicked designs on Louisa.

NOTES AND GLOSSARY:

horse flesh, blind hookey, . . . : a typically Dickensian list of random associations calculated to indicate chaos in business affairs

blind hookey: a card game

a mysterious leg: a humorous way of saying that the old lady had been bedridden for that time

Coriolanian: a descriptive word based on the Shakespearean character Coriolanus, from the play of that name, who was noted for his fierceness and aggression

Royal arms: the heraldic symbols of royalty

Union Jack: the British flag

Magna Charta: Magna Carta, the agreement signed by King John of England in 1215 guaranteeing certain rights to his subjects

John Bull: a symbol of Britain

Habeas Corpus: a legal provision requiring that a person held in custody must be presented to a judge by a certain time for decision as to the legality of his imprisonment

Bill of Rights: a statute passed in England in 1689 after the deposing of King James II

Princes and Lords: the two lines quoted here are from Oliver Goldsmith's (1730–74) famous poem 'The Deserted Village' (1770)

the tumbling-girl: a reference to Sissy and the circus where she would have performed acrobatics

---

Chapter 8: Never Wonder

Dickens once again recapitulates the theme of fact versus fancy and repeats that in Coketown those in charge of education will only accept facts. The populace, though, he points out, naturally seeks to escape from the drudgery of fact. His key examples of the product of a factual education, Tom and Louisa, are found in conversation in this chapter. Tom is bewailing his life and remarking that Sissy Jupe is being treated in the same stultifying manner as he and Louisa. Unlike anyone else, he is able to get Louisa to show some emotion and he exhibits an understanding of Bounderby's designs on her. He tells Louisa that he plans to use this to his own advantage in gaining employment at Bounderby's bank, which he regards primarily as a means of escape from his home. The chapter ends as it began with reflections on the use of the imagination. Louisa is confessing to Tom that she finds some delight in letting her imagination roam. Whilst she is speaking, Mrs Gradgrind enters and expresses concern that after such a scientific education her children should still wish to wonder.

COMMENTARY: There may be some foundation in the charge that Dickens's fertile imagination is showing signs of fatigue at this stage of the novel. It is certainly repetitive in its theme, and in its illustrations of this theme. Also, there is such a sudden change of character in Louisa that we question the artistic judgment at work here. However, it may be that Sissy Jupe's influence is already making itself felt in the Gradgrind household.

The picture of Tom scheming at Louisa's expense comes also rather suddenly—though we might think that there was a suggestion at the conclusion of Chapter 4 of his awareness of the possibilities of capitalising on Bounderby's affection for Louisa. Sudden though it may be, however, it is to prove a vital structural device in the novel.

NOTES AND GLOSSARY:

De Foe: Daniel Defoe (1660–1731), an English author best known for his novels *Robinson Crusoe* and *Moll Flanders*

Euclid: Greek mathematician most noted for his use of logic

Cocker: Edward Cocker (1631–75), an English engraver and schoolmaster known for his copy-book of writing exercises and his book *Cocker's Arithmetic*. The phrase 'according to Cocker' came to mean 'absolutely correct'

Chapter 9: Sissy's Progress

There is an irony in the chapter heading here, for, in terms of the Gradgrind philosophy, Sissy is not making any progress at all. She is caught, as Dickens says, between M'Choakumchild and Mrs Gradgrind. The only thing that keeps her with the Gradgrinds is her firm belief that her father will return. For the first time in the novel she and Louisa talk together, and she tells Louisa of the real love that exists between her and her father. The conversation is interrupted by Tom who urges Louisa to join her father and Bounderby in the drawing-room. He hopes that Louisa will help him curry favour with Bounderby.

COMMENTARY: The plot (like Sissy) makes little progress in this chapter. Dickens uses it to inform us that Sissy's father is still missing, and that the practically-minded Gradgrinds are assured he never will return. The author indicates that Tom's plans are already being set in motion. Further to this, he shows some maturing of Louisa's character in her willingness to listen to the expression of emotion and even to invite it.

NOTES AND GLOSSARY:

whether the Sultan . . . : a reference to the stories of Scheherazade, who, in the *Arabian Nights,* marries the Sultan and saves her life by entertaining him night after night with her tales

---

Chapter 10: Stephen Blackpool

In this chapter we are introduced to a new character in the novel. Stephen Blackpool is one of those thousands of workers who live in Coketown. Though only forty years old, he is, as Dickens says, already an old man. He is seen waiting outside the works for his friend Rachael, a woman of thirty-five; he likes to walk home with her despite the gossiping neighbours. Having walked her to her home and said goodnight, he makes his way to his own lodgings. When he arrives there, he is surprised by the presence of a woman, 'a disabled, drunken creature'. They obviously know one another, though at this point Dickens does not tell us who she is.

COMMENTARY: In this chapter Dickens introduces his sub-plot. It is quickly shown to have narrative links with the main plot, but at this stage has more a melodramatic effect than a structural one. It may be that Dickens suspected his plot was flagging somewhat and needed new interest.

For those familiar with Victorian fiction, the picture of the drunken woman suddenly appearing out of nowhere and obviously having some claim on a man is not unusual. Nor is it unusual for the author, having introduced this strand into his plot, to make his audience wait for further disclosures. It is not difficult, however, to guess who the woman is, given the hint of something forbidden in the relationship between Stephen and Rachael. The latter's encouragement to him to 'Let the laws be' and her earlier statement ''Tis better not to walk too much together' amply show that they are in some way risking a scandal in their association. Stephen and Rachael may be regarded as personifications of the injustices rampant in the industrial world as Dickens sees it. It had been suggested earlier that in this world many people lead miserable lives. In this chapter Dickens singles out two such figures to show what is true of them all. That they provide such evidence is clear from the second paragraph of the chapter—an extended sentence which eventually gives one of these two figures a name: Stephen Blackpool.

Chapter 11: No Way Out

In this chapter Stephen seeks an interview with Bounderby, his employer, to ask his advice on the question of marriage and divorce. Dickens did not keep us waiting too long for clarification. Owing to the strict conditions of his employment, Stephen is forced to use his lunch break as the only chance of seeing Bounderby. Dickens takes this opportunity of contrasting 'the little bread' that Stephen had for his lunch with the more sumptuous meal being enjoyed by his employer. Mrs Sparsit, whom we first met in Chapter Seven, appears here as Bounderby's housekeeper; she witnesses not only his meal but his decisions, too. Indeed, she contributes in this chapter to the sense of moral alarm expressed by Bounderby on hearing of Stephen's wish to be divorced. She and Bounderby between them make it clear to Stephen that there is, as the chapter heading suggests, no way out of his situation.

COMMENTARY: Though Dickens does not keep the modern reader waiting very long for explanation he did in fact make his contemporaries wait a week, for this chapter appeared as the opening one of the next issue of the weekly *Household Words*. The introductory paragraphs of the chapter contain some of the most powerful writing in the book and stand as Dickens's most trenchant condemnation of the working conditions of the 'hands'. The jungle images of serpents and elephants can fruitfully be contrasted with the idyll suggested by Dickens's earlier picture of the circus folk.

A further contrast is afforded by the environment enjoyed by Bounderby and that endured by his workers. There is, too, a virulent strain of irony in the moral indignation expressed by Bounderby and Mrs Sparsit on Stephen's request for advice about divorce. For Dickens has made clear how immoral Bounderby is with reference to the conditions he thinks tolerable for his workers, and we are to see him as the personification of injustice in the society of the day.

NOTES AND GLOSSARY:
Eas'r Monday nineteen year sin: Easter Monday nineteen years ago
played old Gooseberry: created chaos
brigg: bridge
Doctors' Commons: a law court in London at which Dickens was once a reporter

Chapter 12: The Old Woman

Having left Bounderby, Stephen meets an old woman who asks him who lives in the house which he has just left. She establishes that it is Bounderby and asks about his health and appearance. She has come, she tells Stephen, that very day after a long journey—a journey which she makes every year just to catch a glimpse of Bounderby. She seems to have no other interest than that, and certainly makes much of Stephen when she finds he works at Bounderby's mill.

Stephen returns to work to dwell once more on the reality of his miseries which are aggravated by his not being able to see Rachael after work that evening. He makes his way home with a feeling of dread.

COMMENTARY: Dickens introduces yet another mystery at this point in the novel, another carrot, as it were, to dangle before his readers to help to maintain their curiosity. Who, indeed, is this strange woman, and what is her interest in Bounderby? The opening sentence of the second paragraph in this chapter tells us that Stephen had hoped to be consoled by Rachael, and his deep affection for her is made very clear here. She has stood by him all these years waiting patiently for his possible release from his wife. It is a measure of the unrelieved grimness of *Hard Times* that Stephen's dilemma is never happily resolved.

NOTES AND GLOSSARY:

Hummobee: a humming bee

Parliamentary: a train on which the fares were cheaper than normal

patricians: foremost citizens

Divine Right: a reference to the notion that men's affairs are directly ordered by God

Towers of Babel: a reference to the story in the Old Testament in which men sought to defy the Almighty by building their way to heaven. See Genesis 11

Chapter 13: Rachael

Stephen eventually forces himself to go home. There he sees a candle burning in the window and finds Rachael in his room. She is tending his wife, who is desperately ill. Rachael tells him that she must stay and look after his wife as long as she can. She also persuades Stephen to sleep for a while.

In his sleep, Stephen has a terrifying dream in which his wedding day turns into the day of his execution on the gallows. Then, between sleep and waking, he senses that his wife is awake and is stretching her hand towards a bottle of poison near the bed. Stephen, in his present condition, is helpless to do anything, but at the crucial moment

Rachael intervenes and prevents the suicide. The chapter concludes with Rachael's departure, leaving Stephen in charge of his sick wife.

COMMENTARY: Dickens's depiction of Rachael as nurse to Stephen's wife is rich not only in its contribution to our understanding of Rachael's supreme goodness but also in its obviously tragic irony. That she should later be directly instrumental in saving the life of Stephen's wife only accentuates this ironic sense.

Dickens unashamedly provided some familiar signals of impending doom: the storm that Stephen fails even to notice, and the fearful nightmare that torments him in his fitful sleep. There is, despite these tragic effects, a real threat that Dickens will descend to the level of the merely melodramatic, a danger that is increased by his totally adulatory treatment of Rachael.

Chapter 14: The Great Manufacturer

We are re-introduced in this chapter to some of the leading figures in Dickens's main plot, namely, the Gradgrinds and Sissy Jupe. Dickens indicates that some time has passed and that Louisa is now a woman. Sissy has completed her education, and Tom Gradgrind is working for Bounderby. Thomas Gradgrind has been elected to Parliament. Dickens introduces yet another touch of the mysterious by keeping Louisa—as well as his readers—waiting some time for a crucial discussion with her father. But the subject of this discussion is anticipated by Tom, who tells her that Bounderby is involved in some plan with their father. The fact that Mrs Sparsit is not in Bounderby's confidence in this matter offers us a further hint that what he has to say to Gradgrind will involve Louisa.

COMMENTARY: The construction of the novel suffers somewhat at this stage by the insistence that years have passed. The intrusion of the Blackpool episodes does not appear to cover such a time-span convincingly—certainly not enough to make it credible that, in the meanwhile, the Gradgrinds have matured to such a considerable degree. But Dickens must move his plot forward and beg his readers' 'willing suspension of disbelief'.

He still insists on introducing mysterious elements into his plot, and we have already seen that his motive is not so much artistic as pecuniary. He must keep persuading his readers to buy the serial. But Dickens uses some easily recognised features to suggest a degree of unity and coherence in his plot. For example, Tom Gradgrind is still as much a schemer as ever; Louisa still stares into the fire as of old; and Sissy Jupe still has the bottle of oils for soothing her father's aching limbs when he eventually returns to her.

Chapter 15: Father and Daughter

The following morning, Thomas Gradgrind conducts the interview with Louisa in which he acquaints her with Bounderby's proposal of marriage. Louisa proves quite difficult and embarrasses her father by the nature of the questions she asks him. She asks, for example, whether Bounderby will expect her to love him. It is finally made clear that Bounderby only wishes to marry her—there is no immediate demand that she love him. Louisa agrees on these practical terms to marry Bounderby, and the news is communicated to Mrs Gradgrind. Sissy is there at the time and Dickens tells us that from that time the relationship between her and Louisa changes for the worse: Louisa becomes 'impassive, proud, and cold'.

COMMENTARY: Gradgrind's character does not seem to have been developed at all in spite of the hints of maturing and mellowing earlier in the book. Any promise of a development of character in his daughter Louisa seems finally to have been scotched by Dickens's pointed statements at the end of the chapter. Sissy's influence to the good, therefore, has not come to anything so far in the novel. The fruits of Louisa's education are made abundantly clear throughout the chapter; she is the one through whom they are expressed. Indeed, Louisa has obviously taken a much more aggressive stance over the years and pointedly confronts her father with the neglect of the development of any emotional qualities in her make-up. It is something she is to bring more effectively to his notice in her eventual breakdown later in the novel. In the meantime, however, all is presented on a strictly factual base.

There is, despite the grimness, a touch of humour in Dickens's narrative. Gradgrind's anxiety to justify the marriage by reference to the most unlikely statistics—as exemplified in statements about the Calmucks of Tartary—is droll enough; and the 'recumbent' Mrs Gradgrind's unashamed self-centredness and her inane concern about how to address her future son-in-law help to add a kind of melancholy madness to the scene.

NOTES AND GLOSSARY:

Blue Beard:	the villain of a traditional tale, noted for murdering several wives
blue books:	official government reports based on statistics, so called because of their blue covers
Tartary:	the empire established by Ghengis Khan in medieval times in Eastern Europe
Calmucks:	a Mongolian tribe

Chapter 16: Husband and Wife

The plot now moves at a fast pace. What was only a proposal in the previous chapter becomes reality in this one. Bounderby marries Louisa. Before doing so he has had to overcome what to him appeared an embarrassing obstacle: Mrs Sparsit. He does so without any apparent difficulty! She readily congratulates him on his engagement and, equally readily, agrees to move to lodgings over the bank. Agreeable terms are reached, including a private apartment for her there and an annual allowance. Within weeks of his proposal and Louisa's acceptance, they are married and leave England for Lyons in France, for their honeymoon.

COMMENTARY: Dickens's development of the plot is demonstrably compressed here. He did indeed once complain to his friend, Forster, that 'the difficulty of space is crushing', and here it is very much in evidence. He could have made a great deal of the interview between Bounderby and Mrs Sparsit but chooses not to. Instead, he surprises us, as well as Mr Bounderby, by having the lady accept the sudden announcement of his engagement in a totally unperturbed manner. it is not difficult for the reader, though, to sense her rage. Notice the wording of her apparently bland good wishes: 'I fondly hope that Miss Gradgrind may be all you desire, *and deserve*.' She quickly assumes the dominant role in the conversation over the wedding and, indeed, in spite of her eccentricity is now firmly established in the novel as one who will help to shape events. In this she affords an obvious contrast to Mrs Gradgrind, whose passivity is in fact a form of comic, though exasperating, eccentricity.

The interview between Mrs Sparsit and Bounderby is really the central issue in this chapter which contains the marriage of Bounderby and Louisa, and concludes the First Book.

NOTES AND GLOSSARY:

bag and baggage: completely

break the looking glass: an expression of anger

Don't go to the North Pole: Mr Bounderby's exaggerated way of telling Mrs Sparsit to stay near the fire

mittens: gloves without tips on the fingers

bottoms: a reference to ships' bottoms

BOOK THE SECOND: *REAPING*

Chapter 1: Effects in the Bank

A year has passed since the wedding of Bounderby and Louisa. Mrs Sparsit now lives in chambers above the bank. One of the servants in her establishment is Bitzer, the schoolboy of Chapter Two of Book One.

It is a hot summer's afternoon, and Mrs Sparsit is sitting at the window of her room looking over what Dickens calls a 'frying street'. Bitzer is shown to be her spy who reports back to her, particularly on the actions of Tom and Louisa. She still looks down on Bounderby and sees him as a 'victim' of his marriage. Having brought us up-to-date, as it were, Dickens introduces another new character into his novel in the guise of a 'stranger'. He tells Mrs Sparsit and Bitzer that he is looking for Bounderby the banker. Dickens does not give us his name, but the description of his dress and his manner, and the fact that he puts 'no more faith in anything than Lucifer' will indicate to anyone familiar with Dickens that he is up to no good! He has been given a letter of introduction to Bounderby by Gradgrind whom he had met in London.

COMMENTARY: The title of the Second Book is 'Reaping'. That of the First Book, we remember, is 'Sowing'. We have already noted that these titles echo the saying 'As ye sow, so also shall ye reap'. In other words, the deeds you perform at one stage in your life will make their effects felt later, and the usual interpretation is that it is evil deeds that will have to be accounted for later. The plausible stranger who appears in this chapter carries with him a suggestion of this kind of threat for the future. At present, it is a little intangible, but Dickens gives us several hints that justify this feeling. It is the stranger, for example, who says 'Banks, I know, are always suspicious', and the epithet 'suspicious' is almost immediately transferred to him. Several questions can be raised: why has he lost his way to the bank when he is obviously such a capable fellow? Why has he an interest in Louisa? Why is he so intent on impressing Mrs Sparsit whom he flatters unashamedly? He is obviously designed to figure largely in this part of the novel.

Notice how in the third paragraph of this chapter Dickens launches a further attack on the Coketown industrialists. He tells us that whenever government tried to persuade them to improve the conditions for their workers, they simply threatened to close down their factories and thus endanger the economy. In this chapter we are introduced to the notion of union organisation in the novel, a significant force in Dickens's plot.

Chapter 2: Mr James Harthouse

Dickens now divulges the stranger's name, and described his meeting
with Bounderby. It would seem that Harthouse is a man-about-town,
an idler who has tried most things and found them boring. He has been
persuaded by his brother to curry favour with the 'Hard Facts' party of
which Gradgrind is a member. He, it is believed, will give that party a
touch of class; he will be able to 'sell' the party to sections of the public
which it would not normally be able to reach. The plan has worked. He
has successfully ingratiated himself with Gradgrind, who now introduces him to wealth in the person of Bounderby. He would, however,
have quickly tired of this if he had not also been introduced to Louisa,
whom he meets at this point. He finds her both attractive and a challenge to his male ego. In the latter part of this chapter, he has the
opportunity of meeting Tom Gradgrind and sees a way of reaching
Louisa's affections through him.

COMMENTARY: There is not a great deal of subtlety in Dickens's
approach to James Harthouse. A typical member of the self-interested,
spoilt, privileged section of society, Harthouse assumes an air of indifference to anything serious and is unashamed that he has no real and
lasting beliefs or loyalties. Dickens constantly hints at his thinly-
disguised intentions towards Louisa even at this early stage. The
novel's social attack moves away, for the moment, from concentrating
on the economy alone, to the related part played by a corrupt House of
Commons. Here Dickens relates the story of a rail disaster which, by
virtue of the witty eloquence of a parliamentarian, is transformed into
sheer farce.

Dickens does, however, return to his attack on the *laissez-faire* econ-
omists in the ludicrous statements attributed to Bounderby in this
chapter: 'First of all, you see our smoke . . . . It's the healthiest thing in
the world in all respects, and particularly for the lungs.' Dickens is now
employing a rather blunt form of humour to force home his point in as
insistent a manner as the constant whirr of the machines he described in
Chapter One of this Book as having a 'measured motion'.

NOTES AND GLOSSARY:

Graces:	in Greek mythology three sisters who were the per-sonification of charm and beauty in human life. 'Cutting the throats of the Graces' alludes to the violence done to the idea of beauty
Gradgrind school:	not a reference to his educational establishment but to his philosophy or school of thought
yaw-yawed:	imitation of upper-class speech mannerisms

enervated:	exhausted
hybrid race:	a mixture of human kind
epitome:	summary
riff-raff:	rabble
salubrious:	healthy (Dickens is being facetious here)
polonies and saveloys: sausages	

Chapter 3: The Whelp

The 'whelp' is what Dickens, speaking through James Harthouse, calls Tom Gradgrind. A whelp, another name for a young pup, has less attractive connotations when used to describe a human being. It suggests worthlessness and underhandedness. And so it is with Tom who, in the hands of the sophisticated Harthouse, proves malleable putty! This chapter shows how Harthouse gathers information about Louisa, Bounderby, Mrs Sparsit and Gradgrind from the unsuspecting Tom.

Dickens has earlier mentioned Lucifer when speaking of Harthouse. In this chapter, he adopts a similar description: 'he knew himself to be a kind of agreeable demon who had only to hover over him and he must give up his whole soul if required.' Dickens has now introduced and is fast developing a further strand in his story, distinct from the Blackpool/Rachael story, and though related to the Gradgrind/Bounderby strand, still somewhat distinct from that, too.

COMMENTARY: This is probably the most vivid portrayal of Tom in the novel, combining humour with grim reality. The concluding part of the chapter is perhaps the best example of this. The picture of Tom trying to be a 'man of the world' like Harthouse and getting hopelessly drunk in the course of his efforts is very funny. But Dickens's own reflections on the damage Tom had done are grim:

> If he had had any sense of what he had done that night . . . he might have turned short on the road, might have gone down to the ill-smelling river that was dyed black, might have gone to bed in it for good and all . . .

Chapter 4: Men and Brothers

This chapter features the union meeting at which Stephen Blackpool is disciplined for refusing to agree to the negotiating terms formulated by the United Aggregate Tribunal. Dickens emphasises the ranting oratory of Slackbridge, the union representative, and contrasts it with the submissive, humble pleas of Stephen to be allowed to work despite his inability to agree with policy. His workmates refuse to work with him, and he cannot bring himself to seek solace from Rachael. In this loneliness, he is approached by Bitzer, identified here only by the description with which we are already familiar: 'a young man of a very light complexion'. Bitzer tells Blackpool that Bounderby wishes to speak to him.

COMMENTARY: Dickens shows himself to be out of sympathy with the Union orator, Slackbridge. For, though it may be agreed that the union is acting in the men's interests, the means it adopts are shown to be inappropriate. This is best shown, of course, in the harsh treatment meted out to Stephen. The suggestion is that any organisation which acts like this is as inhumane as the system it opposes. Indeed, Dickens regards it as the same in kind as any of those institutions that he took to task earlier in the novel.

Slackbridge is as much a machine as the elephants of the factory—just as they always move with the same monotonous motion, so Slackbridge only ever mops his 'corrugated forehead' in one direction: left to right. Stephen's role as the martyr in this novel continues—first a victim to the institution of marriage, now a victim to his chosen occupation and his views. Dickens is determined to wring as much sympathy out of his readers as possible.

The question is: has he overdone it? Has he, too, exaggerated too much the relationship between the repulsive appearance of Slackbridge and his offensive character? It may be that Dickens is providing here an interesting contrast to his presentation of Harthouse who insinuates himself by virtue of his pleasing appearance. Thus Dickens will have us believe that evil can take many forms.

NOTES AND GLOSSARY:

battened upon: fed like gluttons

axioms: statements of principle

he who sold his birthright for a mess of pottage: a reference to the story in the Old Testament of Esau who gave up his legal rights of property to his brother Jacob for a plateful of stew. See Genesis 25

Judas Iscariot: the disciple who betrayed Jesus Christ

Castlereagh: Robert Stewart Castlereagh (1769–1822), British statesman accused of betraying British interests in Ireland. He eventually committed suicide

liefer: rather

moydert: confused

Strike o' day: dawn

fratch: disagreement

Gonnows: God knows

Brutus:	Marcus Brutus (*c.* 85–42 BC), the Roman politician who took part in the murder of Julius Caesar; the event is the subject of Shakespeare's play *Julius Caesar*
Spartan mothers:	Sparta, a city of ancient Greece, had a long military tradition, and its women were bred to become efficient, unfeeling mothers of soldiers
fugleman:	the soldier who beat time for a drill
sent to Coventry:	disowned and ostracised by workmates

Chapter 5: Men and Masters

As at their last meeting, Stephen again finds Bounderby eating. He is now in the company of his wife, Louisa, and her brother Tom and Harthouse. It is significant that when we meet Harthouse again, on this occasion we find him talking to Louisa. He treats Stephen with indifference. Bounderby demands that Blackpool tell them of his dealings with the union—or Combination as he calls it. Stephen is not to be bullied into volunteering opinions about the Union; on the contrary, he firmly defends the sincerity of most of its members. Stephen does not, in fact, address his remarks to Bounderby but to Louisa in whose face he seems to find some sympathy. Bounderby asks him to explain what the workers have to complain about.

Stephen quite simply points out that there seems no purpose in their lives. They are born to work in terrible conditions, and then just to die. They are not encouraged to have any hopes or aspirations. In anger, Bounderby says he will crush any threat of rebellion by transporting Slackbridge and his kind as convicts. Stephen replies that this kind of action will not solve the underlying problem. He insists that both parties must be prepared to meet, to compromise and thus reach agreement. They must not maintain their extreme, opposing positions. For his speech, Stephen is sacked on the spot by the enraged Bounderby.

COMMENTARY: Stephen's fate grows worse and worse. His plight must now be desperate. He has a drunken wife from whom he cannot escape; he loves Rachael but cannot marry her; he is disowned by his workmates; and now, finally, he is dismissed by his employer. It is because of tragic events such as these that G.K. Chesterton (1874–1936), the novelist and critic, once spoke of *Hard Times* as 'the harshest' of Dickens's stories. This chapter does, however, have one ray of hope in it. It is to be found in the person of Louisa in whom Stephen seems instinctively to find sympathy. In this Dickens hints at some developing sensibility in her. The other two figures in this little drama, Tom and Harthouse, are conspicuously silent, and their silence itself seems ominous.

Chapter 6: Fading Away

On leaving the house, Stephen meets Rachael in the company of the mysterious old lady he had met when he last visited Bounderby at his home. She is anxious to hear of Bounderby's wife, and is delighted to hear that she is 'bonny'. Stephen breaks the news to Rachael that he is finished with Bounderby, and has decided to leave Coketown and seek his fortune elsewhere. He invites Rachael and the old woman back to his room for a cup of tea, and we learn that his wife had left him again some months ago. We also hear that the old woman's name is Mrs Pegler, and that she is a widow who had a son who is now apparently 'dead'.

She appears very perturbed when she hears that a Bounderby has come to see Stephen, but this proves to be Louisa and not Josiah. She is accompanied by Tom. She expresses her concern for Stephen's plight and offers him money. Stephen accepts two pounds, but insists that they are only a loan. He plans to leave the area, he tells them, and seek employment elsewhere. Before Louisa and Tom leave, the latter pulls Stephen urgently out of the room and says he might be able to do him a favour. He tells him to be outside Bounderby's bank at night and wait for an hour or so. He says that if he can help Stephen he will give Bitzer a message for him. He claims that Louisa will agree with what he has in mind, and this single fact seems to persuade Stephen to agree to Tom's request.

Immediately after Tom and Louisa have left, Stephen and Rachael see Mrs Pegler safely to her lodgings, and then they themselves part company. Stephen dutifully spends three nights outside the bank. On the last night, he remains there for over two hours making sure that he is seen by Bitzer in case the latter has a message for him. Nothing happens. The next morning Stephen leaves Coketown alone.

COMMENTARY: The suspicion we had that Louisa's sensibility and sensitivity were developing is confirmed here when she shows considerable understanding of Stephen's plight. Dickens highlights the gap between the two societies of rich and poor in England at this time, by reminding us that this was the first time Louisa had ever had any direct dealing with one of the millions of workers whom she had, till then, only known as statistics.

Mrs Pegler's suspicious reactions to Bounderby's name is Dickens's way of telling us that there is some kind of relationship there yet to be uncovered. The fact, too, that she says she had a child but had 'lost him' leads us to believe that Bounderby is her son. We must, however, wait for some time before we receive real confirmation of this fact.

We must wait, too, for the outcome of Tom's obviously devious plot involving Stephen. He says that Bounderby might have a message for him, but it becomes obvious that Bounderby is totally unaware of this. Why, then, has Tom arranged for Stephen to loiter outside the bank at night, making sure that he is easily seen by the arch-spy, Bitzer? A hint is offered as to Tom's purpose in this sentence: 'Stephen even began to have an uncomfortable sensation upon him of being for the time a disreputable character.'

NOTES AND GLOSSARY:

Lord Chesterfield: an English statesman (1694–1773) best remembered for his *Letters to his Son* offering advice and worldly wisdom

---

Chapter 7: Gunpowder

In this chapter Dickens deals with the developing relationship between Louisa and Harthouse. They are often in one another's company—though, as Dickens points out, neither of them has any ulterior motive in this. Louisa sees their relationship in the light of an attitude that she has developed, namely, 'What did anything matter?' and Harthouse sees it as all part of the 'great fun' that was his object in life.

They meet at a new residence taken over by Bounderby from a bankrupt. It is fifteen miles outside Coketown and set in beautiful surroundings. It is Harthouse's prime intention to gain some kind of response from Louisa. He sees that the best way to do this is to show interest in her brother. So, in his talks with her, he comes straight to the point and expresses concern that Tom may have gambling debts. Louisa agrees that this may be so, and even volunteers the information that Tom has borrowed large sums of money from her. Harthouse expresses sympathy for Tom, saying that his upbringing has really proved a disadvantage to him as he has no one to turn to except his sister. At the same time, Harthouse says that Tom has not duly recognised how much he owes his sister. He ought to demonstrate some love and regard for her. It is his intent, he says, to help Tom himself and, having done so, to be in a better position to insist that he treats Louisa more kindly.

At this point, they see Tom himself coming towards them in an obvious temper. Harthouse calms him down and, once Louisa has left them, has a confidential chat with him. He learns that Tom is annoyed that Louisa does not exercise enough influence on Bounderby to get him more money. He actually breaks down and cries, and Harthouse takes the chance to invite him to confide in him as a friend. He also persuades Tom to be more loving to his sister. In this way Harthouse has effectively won the affections of both brother and sister.

COMMENTARY: Despite Dickens's assertions that Harthouse is only out to enjoy himself, it is made clear that in doing so Harthouse is putting others in jeopardy. As the final paragraph of the chapter shows, Louisa's long and lasting devotion to Tom has already grown 'much the less' because of her interest in Harthouse.

Tom is presented here much more as a victim—a victim not only of his upbringing and environment but also of the schemer Harthouse. We have been accustomed to see Tom as a schemer but Harthouse can outwit him. Just as Dickens was intent on showing us the developing sensibilities in Louisa, so here, in the tearful Tom, he shows some growing awareness.

NOTES AND GLOSSARY:

Gorgon: in Greek mythology there were three Gorgons, sisters, whose heads were covered with snakes instead of hair and who, if looked upon, could turn a man to stone

Westminster School: the English public school attached to Westminster Abbey

King's Scholar: holder of a scholarship awarded to pupils of high intellectual achievement

---

Chapter 8: Explosion

The aptness of the title of this chapter becomes obvious when Bounderby tells Harthouse that the bank has been robbed. Bounderby's intention of causing Harthouse alarm by his dramatic announcement fails and Harthouse points out that he was lucky that only one hundred and fifty pounds has gone. Bounderby, however, is not to be calmed. Having been joined by Louisa, Mrs Sparsit and Bitzer, he relates how the money was stolen from Tom Gradgrind's safe the previous night. He says more would have been stolen but the thief had been disturbed. He had made his entrance, it would appear, using a false key. Tom, he says, is being interviewed by the police, but the suspect is, in fact, Stephen Blackpool. Harthouse, surprisingly enough, makes a guess at this himself. Bounderby says that Blackpool was seen loitering outside the bank at night. There is, though, a second suspect, namely, an old woman who was seen in his company, and who has also been seen watching the bank during the day.

At this point, there is an amusing brief interlude in which Dickens describes Mrs Sparsit's behaviour in the house. Her main intention is to cause discomfort to Louisa whom she insists on calling Miss Gradgrind. It is she, for example, who draws attention to the fact that Louisa and Harthouse are in the garden together in the evening.

The last part of the chapter deals with Louisa's questioning of Tom, who has returned from Coketown on the 'mail train'. She obviously suspects him of the robbery and begs him to confess to her. He pretends not to understand what she means. However, his actions when he is left alone in his bedroom will persuade the reader that he is indeed guilty.

COMMENTARY: Mrs Sparsit is now assuming a role of some significance. Suddenly transported to Bounderby's country house, she immediately begins to impose her will on both him and Louisa. She throws suspicion on Louisa's connection with Harthouse, and calls into question her role as a wife. All this is of a piece with the general cynicism with which Dickens regards the various characters that appear in this and the previous chapter. Only Louisa is left unscathed as she shows concern for both Stephen Blackpool and Tom.

Dickens's concern with the jigsaw plotting of his novel which is working so well is reflected in the many schemes and plots devised by his various characters: Tom Gradgrind's designs on Blackpool and the bank, Harthouse's on Louisa, Mrs Sparsit's on Louisa and on Bounderby.

NOTES AND GLOSSARY:

legion: possibly a reference to the story in the New Testament of the man possessed by a devil calling himself Legion (Mark 5: 9). This would be in keeping with Dickens's depiction of Harthouse as some kind of evil spirit

the Devil . . . lion: a direct reference to the first Epistle of the Apostle Peter in the New Testament: 'the devil, as a roaring lion, walketh about, seeking whom he may devour' (1 Peter 5: 8)

flying into town on a broomstick: Bounderby speaks of the old lady as though she were a witch

a mangle: an old-fashioned device consisted of two rollers turned by a handle and used for smoothing linen

lambent: descriptive of a light playing on a surface without burning it

backgammon: a board game played with counters and dice

Chapter 9: Hearing the Last of it

The opening of the chapter deals with the growing rift between Bounderby and Louisa, a rift engineered skilfully and deliberately by Mrs Sparsit. Dickens, though, distracts us from this line of the plot by whisking Louisa off to Coketown where her mother is dying. There, looking after her, she finds her sister Jane and Sissy. Mr Gradgrind, Dickens tells us, is not there but is in the 'national dustyard', that is, Parliament. Alone, Louisa witnesses the death of her mother.

COMMENTARY: Dickens's death scenes enjoy a considerable literary reputation. There is in them a sensitivity of feeling that is unspoilt by any sense of exaggeration' or ridicule. This effect of sensitivity is beautifully caught in a simple phrase: 'the light that had always been feeble and dim behind the weak transparency, went out.' After the rush, bother and disturbance of the recent chapters, Mrs Gradgrind's death is, ironically, something of a respite. Louisa's response to her mother's death is offered as further evidence of her growing sensibilities: she kisses her frail hand. As if to demonstrate what benefits would have accrued from Louisa's continuing relationship with Sissy, Dickens shows how Jane has prospered under her influence.

NOTES AND GLOSSARY:
consummate velocity: high speed
epigrammatically: wittily and concisely

Chapter 10: Mrs Sparsit's Staircase

Mrs Sparsit stays on at Bounderby's and continues to spy on Louisa. We learn that so far Blackpool and the 'old woman' have not been found. Meanwhile Harthouse tries to convince Louisa that Stephen Blackpool was exactly the kind of person to have committed the robbery: he had, as the jargon has it, motive and opportunity.

COMMENTARY: The crucial item in this chapter is Dickens's insistence on Mrs Sparsit's staircase. It refers directly, of course, to the phenomenon spoken of in the previous chapter whereby Mrs Sparsit could negotiate staircases in her role as a spy 'with consummate velocity'. Here, though, the staircase has become, as Dickens says, an allegory, a symbol. In her mind's eye, Mrs Sparsit likes to imagine an endless staircase which Louisa constantly descends, making her doom ever more painful and ever more inevitable. The descent is not literal, of course, but refers to the moral decline implicit in her continued relationship with Harthouse.

NOTES AND GLOSSARY:
retreat: a reference to Bounderby's country house—a place to escape to, as it were, away from the dirty Coketown
anchorite: a hermit
Mohammedan persuasion: belief in Mohammed the prophet (*c.* 570—632)

To hear is to obey: Mohammed's response to God's call

allegorical fancy: an imaginative picture (in this case of a staircase) which acts as a symbol

Romulus and Remus: the legendary founders and rulers of Rome, supposed to have been abandoned at birth and then found and nurtured by a she-wolf

Alderney: one of the Channel Islands famous for its breed of cows. Bounderby suggests that just as an Alderney cow is prolific in its milk production so his grandmother was unstinting in dispensing blows and bruises

under the rose: secretly

Chapter 11: Lower and Lower

Mrs Sparsit's insane jealousy of Louisa has now reached dramatic proportions. The chapter deals in detail with her frenetic attempts to spy on Louisa and Harthouse. But they are not so frenzied that they cannot be calculating. She learns from Tom that he is due to meet Harthouse at the station on his return from Yorkshire. At the same time, she learns that Bounderby is not to be at home that same weekend. She anticipates that a plan has been laid by Harthouse to meet Louisa at the house, and this suspicion is confirmed when, spying on Tom, she sees that Harthouse has not arrived at the station to meet him. She sets off immediately to Bounderby's house and there, as she hides in the shrubbery in the garden, she witnesses the encounter between Harthouse and Louisa. It starts to rain heavily, and the couple part. Mrs Sparsit guesses they have a further assignation and decides to follow Louisa. This entails pursuing Louisa to Coketown, travelling in the same train. But, once at Coketown, Louisa disappears.

COMMENTARY: One criticism that can be made of this chapter is that Dickens has descended to mere melodrama. Certainly the vision of this evil-minded woman, Mrs Sparsit, adopting the role of *voyeur* (someone who obtains pleasure from witnessing the private activities of others secretly) is close to the effect of melodrama. In justification of Dickens's depiction, it can be suggested that in presenting such an extreme action taken by Louisa, the author is vividly illustrating how the extreme suppression she suffered as a child could result in an equally extreme reaction. We are thus torn between charging Dickens with artistic ineptitude and attributing to him some quite sophisticated psychological insight. Mrs Sparsit demonstrates in this chapter Dickens's intention of giving her a fuller role than normally offered to one of his eccentric female characters.

NOTES AND GLOSSARY:

apostrophizing: making a speech to, addressing directly in a rhetorical fashion

small fry: literally small, young fish, but here the less important people in the factory

Furies: in Greek mythology these are female figures who tortured the conscience of evil-doers

umbrageous: shady—here, shaded by trees

Chapter 12: Down

The literalness of this chapter's heading is made clear in the last sentence of the chapter: 'And he laid her down there, and saw the pride of his heart and the triumph of his system, lying, an insensible heap, at his feet.' This is a dramatic conclusion to the Second Book, and it comes as the climax to Louisa's heart-searching confession to her father. For it is to her father's house that Louisa has gone, not, as Mrs Sparsit suspected, to the arms of Harthouse. Once there, Louisa accuses her father of neglecting the real needs of her heart and soul in her upbringing. All that Gradgrind can say in his defence is that he did not know that she was unhappy!

COMMENTARY: Dickens was intensely interested in the theatre, both as a writer and as an actor. This scene, with its lengthy dialogue only interrupted by what are, largely, stage directions, exemplifies how the dramatic form has intruded on the novel. Again, it has very much the tone of Victorian melodrama but this is offset by the genuine poignancy of Gradgrind's response to Louisa's affliction. The realisation of her plight comes to him and persuades him to offer positive sympathy. This development is aptly caught in the sentence: 'Her father might instinctively have loosened his hold, but that he felt her strength departing from her.' The scales have fallen from his eyes. There is now a new paternal instinct stirring in him which is challenging the heartless statistics. This change of heart offers a striking contrast to the Gradgrind whom we met at the beginning of both this chapter and the novel.

NOTES AND GLOSSARY:

Good Samaritan: a reference to the New Testament story (Luke 10: 30–5) wherein a man gave help to a stranger in need

BOOK THE THIRD: *GARNERING*

Chapter 1: Another Thing Needful

This chapter depicts the struggle in Louisa's mind. Years of training in restraining herself and repressing her emotions have made it difficult for her to experience any feelings for her father or Sissy or her sister, Jane. Her father's appeals to her threaten to fall even now on deaf ears. Dickens tells us that 'he would have been glad to see her in tears', but the tears will not come. She visibly resists Sissy's good influence and sees her as an enemy. It is only when Sissy's tears touch Louisa's cheeks that she finds in herself the gift of tears and breaks down, held against Sissy's 'loving heart'.

COMMENTARY: An aphorism from this chapter helps to substantiate the suggestion in the commentary on Chapter Eleven of Book the Second that Dickens is capable of astute psychological insight: 'All closely imprisoned forces rend and destroy.' We witness Louisa's struggle with such forces in an effort to find a new self. The emotion is handled delicately and sympathetically by the author, whilst at the same time he shows the reality of her deep-seated resentment of Sissy. Louisa is not the only one who ultimately gains by her harrowing experience, for Thomas Gradgrind himself confesses to a change of heart and, far from being arrogant and dictatorial, he is now subdued and humble.

NOTES AND GLOSSARY:
excise-rod: the device used by excise officers in measuring liquids such as whisky and other spirits

Chapter 2: Very Ridiculous

This chapter takes up the story of the bemused Harthouse. He is visibly disturbed by the unexplained absence of Louisa. He searches for her and questions Tom about her whereabouts. Tom is uncharacteristically aggressive and points out that he has experienced considerable annoyance himself in waiting to meet Harthouse at the station the previous evening.

That night Harthouse has a visit from Sissy who persuades him that he will never see Louisa again and encourages him to leave the district. After a token protest, Harthouse agrees to do so, and, leaving a note for Bounderby and Gradgrind, 'he...left the tall chimneys of Coketown behind'.

COMMENTARY: Our credulity may be stretched a little too far in this chapter. Having witnessed the way in which Harthouse has thrown all caution to the winds in his attempted seduction of Louisa, we may well find it difficult to accept that he would be so accommodating to Sissy when she requests him to leave Coketown and never see Louisa again. In fact, he yields almost instantly to her request, and even repents of being the cause of so much unhappiness.

In a lengthy speech he tells her that he has 'glided on from one step to another with a smoothness so perfectly diabolical'. It may be that Dickens saw that he had exhausted the possibilities of this element in his plot. It may also be yet further substantiation of the angelic influence of Sissy which is really making itself felt in this last Book of the novel.

NOTES AND GLOSSARY:

Holy Office and slow torture: a reference to the workings of the Spanish Inquisition in the fifteenth and sixteenth centuries; it tried and tortured heretics

ingenuousness: innocence

addled eggs: bad eggs that produce no young

Chapter 3: Very Decided

Mrs Sparsit, a shadow of her former self, seeks out Mr Bounderby in London and tells him her tale. Having done this, she faints from exhaustion. In dramatic style, Bounderby whisks her back to Coketown and up to Stone Lodge for a confrontation with Thomas Gradgrind. The latter takes the wind out of their sails, though, by acknowledging that he knows the story already and is able to set the record straight.

When Bounderby hears of Louisa's flight from Harthouse to her father he turns on Mrs Sparsit and demands an apology. She bursts into tears and he packs her off abruptly back to the bank.

Things happen at great speed after this. Bounderby attacks Thomas Gradgrind's protective attitude towards Louisa and lays down an ultimatum, that if she is not at home with him by noon the next day she need never return. The outcome is that, since Louisa fails to meet the dead-line, he 'resumed a bachelor life', as Dickens puts it.

COMMENTARY: The Harthouse episode is well and truly closed. He has already gone and now the after-effects of his actions are seen. Dickens's art in making his plot cohere so well is seen again in this chapter by his referring us back to the much earlier interview between Bounderby and Stephen Blackpool. There, Bounderby had indicated that the severing of ties between man and wife was unthinkable. Dickens asks us to bear this in mind when Bounderby cuts the knot himself on the ground of 'incompatibility'.

This is a beautifully achieved chapter in its clear and believable presentation of the new Thomas Gradgrind. He has obviously come to 'doubt whether I understood Louisa'. There is no false humility in his feelings, no sentimental appeal for sympathy, but simply a reasoned and calm recognition of the need for humanity.

NOTES AND GLOSSARY:

combustibles: things that catch fire easily—a cross reference to Book 2, Chapter 7, 'Gunpowder'

Rocket: reference to George Stephenson's (1781–1848) steam engine 'The Rocket' which he built in 1829

jerk of the hayfield: Dickens has already described Bounderby's head of hair as being like a hayfield—so here he means 'a jerk of the head'. You may remember that Dickens had originally described him as almost bald!

Chapter 4: Lost

Stephen Blackpool's whereabouts suddenly become the focus of attention. Bounderby, with renewed energy since his rift with Louisa, offers a reward of twenty pounds for his 'apprehension'. This gives rise in the first place to a further denunciation of Bounderby by Slackbridge, and, in the second place, to an outburst by Rachael. She protests Stephen's innocence to Bounderby and tells him of the visit to Stephen's lodgings of Tom and Louisa. Bounderby insists that she and Tom should see Louisa at Stone Lodge with him and gain corroberation of Rachael's story.

Despite obvious hints from Tom when they reach Stone Lodge, Louisa does confirm Rachael's account. We learn that Stephen Blackpool has changed his name and that Rachael has been writing to him under that assumed name. She assures them that Stephen will return to Coketown within two days. But Stephen does not return. Rachael is forced to tell of his whereabouts, and messengers are sent to bring him back. He is not, however, to be found.

COMMENTARY: Dickens adopts a daring narrative technique here. Whilst he appears to be tying up loose ends by dealing with the sub-plot he has the audacity to introduce yet another complication. Stephen's reappearance at this point would have solved the problem of the robbery. Instead, Dickens has him disappear mysteriously, and so delays the solution of that particular problem.

The episode involving Tom and Louisa helps to confirm for us Louisa's change of heart, for she refuses to lie for Tom. As for him, he is becoming almost ill with feverish anxiety. His father, too, is looking 'grey and old'. The innocent Rachael, on the other hand, is spoken of as a 'young woman'.

Chapter 5: Found

Blackpool's whereabouts are still not known, and Rachael's only explanation for this is that he may have been murdered. Sissy suggests that he may have fallen ill when making his way back, but Rachael replies that this has been suggested already and all the possible places where he might be found have been searched.

Whilst walking together they witness a commotion outside Bounderby's house. At the centre of it is Mrs Sparsit who is in the process of dragging an old woman out of a coach in which she has been brought from the railway station. She is hustled into Bounderby's house, followed by Rachael and Sissy and a great many of the townspeople. There, in a triumphant moment, Mrs Sparsit delivers the old woman, who was thought to be Stephen's accomplice, to Bounderby. He is, however, none too pleased and asks her 'Why don't you mind your own business, ma'am?'. For the old woman, it would appear, is actually his mother.

Gradgrind, who is also present, rounds on the old woman and abuses her for her neglect of her son as a child—a story Bounderby has persistently related throughout the novel. She is horrified by this, and denies the truth of it vehemently. Bounderby is rightly embarrassed by Mrs Pegler's true account and orders everyone out of his house.

COMMENTARY: The chapter heading might well have persuaded us that it was Stephen who had, at last, been found. Instead, Dickens uses the chapter to tie up one more loose end in his story and at the same time add to Bounderby's humiliation.

One surprising element in this episode is that Gradgrind is still on such friendly terms with Bounderby. We might have thought that the changed and chastened Gradgrind would by now have seen through Bounderby's hypocrisy. Instead, it is he who champions Bounderby against his 'irresponsible' mother until the true facts of the matter come to light.

NOTES AND GLOSSARY:
Slough of Despond: a place of despair described by John Bunyan (1628–88) in his *Pilgrim's Progress* (1678)

Chapter 6: The Starlight

On the Sunday following the discovery of Mrs Pegler, Sissy and Rachael go for a walk about seven miles from Coketown. They are in green countryside which, however, still shows the scars of industry in the shape of deserted mines. It is, indeed, into one of these pits that Stephen has fallen. Sissy first discovers his hat lying on the gound. Rachael becomes hysterical. Sissy has to calm her sufficiently to persuade her to run for help.

Meanwhile Sissy organises a search party to look for Stephen in Old Hell Shaft. It takes four hours for the rescue operation to get fully under way. There are then almost two hundred spectators. Two men are lowered into the pit, and news comes through that Stephen is still alive but so badly hurt that he can not easily be moved. Eventually, however, he is raised to the surface. Once there, he has the chance to speak to Rachael, Louisa and Thomas Gradgrind. He still insists that it is 'aw a muddle', but that he has come to be resigned to that. He asks Gradgrind to clear his name, and, holding Rachael's hand, he dies.

COMMENTARY: Dickens seems to relish this opportunity for an action-packed chapter, and makes the most of it. It opens on a deliberately quiet scene and then simply explodes. He prepares us for the tragedy by mentioning the existence of disued pits, but it still comes as a shock when, with the discovery of Stephen's hat, the awful realisation of his fate overwhelms Rachael. Dickens's means of 'disposing' of Stephen is an economical device. It explains easily his apparent failure to respond to Rachael's letter, it solves the difficulty about divorce, it creates a rosy aura of goodness surrounding the dying and forgiving Stephen. George Eliot (1819–80) another Victorian novelist, uses the same technique to rid herself of Dunstan Cass, a troublesome character in other ways, in her novel *Silas Marner* (1861). Her device is a little more horrific, for Dunstan's skeleton is all that is eventually found! Dickens's treatment has a poignancy that helps to compensate for the relative crudity of the event as a device in the plot.

NOTES AND GLOSSARY:

Fire-damp: The name given by miners to carburetted hydrogen which is explosive when mixed with air.

Chapter 7: Whelp-hunting

In the first part of this chapter we learn that Gradgrind realises Tom's responsibility for Stephen's death and loss of good name. We also discover that Sissy has alerted Tom and helped him to escape, by encouraging him to join Sleary's circus. The circus happens to be within reach of the port of Liverpool, and so Tom could escape from the country by ship. Thomas Gradgrind, Louisa and Sissy go their separate ways in search of Tom. Sissy and Louisa are the first to find Sleary's circus. Tom has been disguised as a black servant in one of the acts and is unrecognisable. Mr Gradgrind arrives an hour later and arrangements are made to get Tom to Liverpool. Before this can be effected, however, Bitzer bursts in on the scene and arrests Tom.

COMMENTARY: In this chapter Dickens effects one of his most telling pieces of irony, and, in a superb *tour de force*, turns fortune's wheel full circle. For the circus that aroused so much contempt in Gradgrind at the beginning of the novel is seen at last to be the one hope of salvation for his son.

Dickens's concern for continuity and coherence in his novel has been stressed already; here we have perhaps the finest example of the success of that concern. The choice of Bitzer to place an arresting arm on Tom is, perhaps, too much of a coincidence. But while it may be seen as a flaw in one respect, it does help to emphasise Dickens's design, his plan for the novel.

NOTES AND GLOSSARY:

down wells: an ironic picture in view of the events of the previous chapter—it means here, though, stair-wells, at the bottom of steep staircases

postilion: outrider of a horse-drawn carriage

kicking a horse in a fly: the old man is kicking the horse which is supposed to draw the carriage (the fly)

turnpike-road: a road on which tolls must be paid

grown too maturely turfy: he had grown a beard!

Chapter 8: Philosophical

When it seems that all hope of escape for Tom is lost Sleary devises another plan. Pretending to sympathise with Bitzer's point of view, he offers to take him with Tom to the railway station. But the horse that draws the carriage in which they ride has been trained to dance, and Sleary's dog has been ordered to detain Bitzer. The plan is that when the horse begins dancing Tom will know that a pony-gig is due to pass. When that happens he is to jump from the carriage and get into the gig which will take him to safety. Bitzer will be prevented from pursuing him by Sleary's dog. The horse will go on dancing for as long as Sleary wishes.

Thus Tom makes his escape. For this service, Sleary accepts some small rewards from Thomas Gradgrind. In talking of his own dog, Sleary is prompted to tell Gradgrind of the sudden and unexpected appearance of Sissy Jupe's dog, Merrylegs. Jupe himself is never heard of again, and Sleary thinks it certain that he is dead.

COMMENTARY: A delightfully Dickensian solution to one of the final problems of the book. What other author would transform the tragic

and the serious so quickly into the near-ludicrous with such panache?
A dancing horse and a prancing dog are the final instruments in Tom's
escape. The menace of Bitzer is transformed into circus antics.
Dickens's solution approaches the incredible. And yet, who can deny
its appropriateness? It is not altogether unlikely that such devoted
animals could perform such feats!

The part played by Sleary's dog is expertly used by Dickens to introduce the topic of Jupe's dog and its fidelity. Through this device
Dickens is able to inform us of the death and final exit from his novel
of yet another character. He is not allowing his characters in this book
merely to slip away. He is intent on accounting for all their fates.

NOTES AND GLOSSARY:

Harvey: William Harvey (1578–1657), an English
anatomist who discovered the circulation of the
blood

Chapter 9: Final

Mrs Sparsit falls from her exalted position when Bounderby discharges
her without any ceremony, and she has to seek refuge under the roof of
her 'relation, Lady Scadgers'. Having dealt with her, Dickens offers us
a look into the future of each of his leading characters. Mr Bounderby
did, in fact, give Bitzer Tom's place in the bank, and made a will offering certain bequests to glorify his own name. Dickens ruefully comments that the law would make due profit out of the contesting of his
will. Gradgrind grows to old age having renounced his factual
approach to life and given up Parliament. Louisa helps her father to
exonerate Stephen Blackpool; she never remarries, but lives quietly,
helping her fellow-men. Rachael, for her part, continues working and,
ironically, helps to support Stephen's wife on her occasional drunken
visits to Coketown. Tom Gradgrind, thousands of miles away,
becomes a reformed character and learns the value of humanity. He
starts on a journey back to England, but dies of a fever on the way.
Sissy Jupe becomes the happy mother of happy children.

COMMENTARY: Victorian readers were often provided with such com-
forting epilogues where the future lives of leading characters were outlined. Dickens adopts the same technique here as a way of rounding off
his narrative, ensuring that none of his characters is forgotten. Indeed,
if we thought he had forgotten the major cause of Stephen's troubles,
here she is reeling once more into Dickens's sad tale to remind us of the
hard times!

Part 3

Commentary

Dickens the novelist

The Victorian period is often thought of as the high-water mark of the novel, and Dickens himself has long been acknowledged as one of the supreme masters of the art.

strengths *1.* His strengths indeed are many. In the first place, he can spin a wonderful yarn. His inventiveness is prodigious. He can weave plots of such complexity as to ensure a sense of mystery and uncertainty all along the way. This, of course, was a necessary facility in a novelist whose many works were produced in serial form. Dickens devoted particular energies to his production of novels of quite bewildering length in an endeavour to please and satisfy the reading public which was apparently never sated in its demand for novels. He had to develop the technique of suspense to a fine art.

2. A further quality of Dickens's invention is his gift of fascinating characterisation. His plots are admired as the product of a fertile and active imagination, yet it might be argued that his greatest achievement lies in the creation of his characters which are vividly and cogently drawn, and invite us warmly into the pages of his books.

3. A third facet of Dickens's achievement in his novels is his gift of humour. Whilst this feature is closely connected with that of characterisation, it is also true to say that Dickens humour is of a more varied kind than would be suggested by character depiction alone. The many instances of facetious authorial comment, the large comic scenes of simple confusion, the sheer wit of dialogue and repartee, are all part of the rich vein of humour that makes Dickens's novels unmistakably his own.

Dickens's novels, however, are not merely good fun. He has a considerable reputation as satirist and critic of society. He takes those institutions respected by the Victorians and exposes their inadequacies and failings; and his satire strikes home and leaves its mark. He attacks Parliament, marriage and the family, philanthropic societies, education, the law and the Church. In 1841, he wrote to his friend and biographer, Forster, 'How radical I am getting'.

What has been written so far has been very much a positive estimate of Dickens's novels. There have been less flattering and more negative assessments, and, for our present particular purposes, it is useful to be

weaknesses

aware of these in relation to *Hard Times*. Lord Macaulay (1800–59), for example, the great English man of letters and historian, spoke of *Hard Times* in these terms in his Journal of 12 August 1854: 'One excessively touching, heart-breaking passage, and the rest sullen socialism. The evils which he attacks he caricatures grossly, and with little humour.' In even harsher terms, the critic Richard Simpson (1820–76) writing for the literary journal *The Rambler* described *Hard Times* thus: 'the story is stale, flat, and unprofitable; a mere dull melodrama in which character is caricature, sentiment tinsel, and moral (if any) unsound.'

Even where Dickens had his champions, they were aware of the shortcomings that provoked adverse criticism. Thus, John Ruskin (1819–1900), a notable English critic, could acknowledge that his view of *Hard Times* need not be shared by all: 'The usefulness of that work (to my mind the greatest he has ever written) is with many persons seriously diminished because Mr Bounderby is a dramatic monster, instead of a characteristic example of a worldly master; and Stephen Blackpool a dramatic perfection instead of a characteristic of an honest workman.'

Evidently a lively debate followed the appearance of the novel, concerned with its literary qualities. Dickens himself was aware of the pressures on him and anxious not to be criticised as producing a work of inferior literary quality. He was used, for example, to monthly serialisation, yet in *Hard Times* he was forced to supply weekly instalments. We know that he was persuaded to write the book in this way to help revive the rapidly dropping sales of his journal *Household Words*. The novel had to run weekly for five months—quite an undertaking. He was concerned that he should not be regarded as a writer merely concerned with sales, profits and topicality. For example, it is claimed that *Hard Times* was born of the Preston strike of 1854 which Dickens briefly witnessed. He was at pains to discount this claim, for he saw it as a threat to his literary reputation; thus he wrote to a friend Peter Cunningham (1816–67):

> The mischief of such a statement is twofold. First it encourages the public to believe in the impossibility that books are produced in that very sudden and cavalier manner . . . and secondly in this instance it has this bearing: it localises . . . a story which has a direct purpose in reference to the working people all over England, and it will cause, as I know by former experience, characters to be fitted onto individuals whom I never saw or heard in my life.

It remains true, however, that the book was born of necessity and that it did, indeed, prove an immediate commercial success.

Is Dickens's credibility as a serious writer, then, in question here?

There are certain indications that this was the case, certainly. For example, in *Hard Times* Dickens appears to abuse the industrialists of his time both in their attitudes towards life and humanity, and in the monstrous factories that they create:

> In the hardest working part of Coketown; in the innermost fortifications of that ugly citadel, where Nature was as strongly bricked out as killing airs and gases were bricked in . . . (p.102)

This picture recurs throughout the novel. Yet only a year earlier, in *Household Words* itself, Dickens had written in praise of industrialists and in a speech in the same year, 1853, had praised both them and their cities! Dickens's friend and biographer, Forster, may well have been aware of this inconsistency when writing of *Hard Times* in the *Examiner* of 9 September 1854. There he suggested that we ought not to look at the novel as a kind of documentary. We must look to it for its appeal to sentiment and not to reason:

> The story is not meant to do what fiction cannot do—to prove a case; its utmost purpose is to express forcibly a righteous sentiment. To run anywhere into a discussion of detail would have checked the current of the tale, which, as it stands, does not flag for the space even of a page. Wherever in the course of it any playful handling of a nation of the day suited the artist's purpose, the use made of it has been artistic always, never argumentative.

In his speech of 6 January 1853, Dickens had said that 'Literature had turned happily' to 'that great phalanx of the people by whose industry, perseverance, and intelligence, and their result in money-wealth, such places as Birmingham and many others like it, have arisen.' It is difficult to equate these sentiments with his depictions of Coketown to which, surely, literature did not turn 'happily'. And it is difficult to see how Forster's view can be made compatible with that of John Ruskin, who was of the mind that '*Hard Times* should be studied with close and earnest care by persons interested in social questions.'

Structure and plot

The structure was dictated to some extent by the serial form in which the novel was initially written. The novel has been praised for its economy of form, that is, for the neat and compact way in which Dickens has organised the narrative. While he is often accused of creating a 'sprawling' novel, here he obviously pays a good deal of attention to coherence. The choice of the titles of the three books indicates a desire to draw attention to this coherence, to make the reader aware of continuity, of cause and effect, of interdependence.

The individual titles with their agricultural connotations are directly related to the theme of personal growth which plays an important part in the novel. The seeds are sown in education and nurture; various persons begin to reap the results, good or bad; and in Book Three Dickens gathers all the various parts together.

The plot is a simple delight. One considerable achievement in *Hard Times* is the way in which Dickens has effected the interrelationships in all the lives of the characters involved. Paths cross and criss-cross with impressive ease and naturalness, and they do so without stretching our credulity too far. Even where such complexity may appear arbitrary and superfluous to the story it proves to contribute to its meaning in the end. Thus, for example, the meeting of Mrs Pegler with Stephen outside Bounderby's house in Chapter 12 of Book One, and again in Chapter 6 of Book Two, proves crucial to Tom's plan of robbing the bank. Their being seen in the same place, both doing the same thing, namely, keeping their eye on the bank, is part of a pattern which persuades us to accept the idea that they could be seen as accomplices. Dickens seems to delight in having his apparently minor characters like Mrs Pegler and Bitzer become involved in the main stream of its events. In many of his other novels, such minor characters would often disappear without a trace. This, indeed, is the fate that threatens Stephen's wife, but even she is credibly resurrected in the finale. It is for these qualities of the plot that one champion of Dickens's claims to consideration as a careful novelist, F.R. Leavis (1895–1975), has singled out *Hard Times* for special praise: 'of all Dickens' works it is the one that has all the strength of his genius together with a strength no other of them can show—that of a completely serious work of art.'

Themes

Dickens's intentions as far as the theme of *Hard Times* is concerned were well summarised by Edwin P. Whipple:

> During the composition of *Hard Times* the author was evidently in an embittered state of mind in respect to social and political questions. He must have felt that he was in some degree warring against the demonstrated laws of the production and distribution of wealth; yet he also felt that he was putting into prominence some laws of the human heart which he supposed political economists had studiously overlooked or ignored. (*Atlantic Monthly*, March 1877)

In the opening chapters of his novel, Dickens investigates the premises on which much of the education of the day seems to have been based. There would appear to have been too much emphasis on the acquisition of facts and a total neglect of the development of sensibility. The grim picture Dickens draws of the environment of the school and home does much to persuade us that such early experience will bear no good fruit in adult life.

He contrasts this with the colourful and rich life of the imagination as experienced by the circus folk. When one of them is subjected to the rigours of Gradgrind's educational philosophy her human nature naturally rejects the attacks made on it: Sissy Jupe learns nothing from the artificially imposed educative processes familiar in the Gradgrind household. But, as we see later in the novel, her own essential goodness is instrumental in educating those suffering from the inadequacies of the Gradgrind philosophy. The central theme of the novel is the conflict of Fact and Fancy in children's education. Where failure occurs in adult life it is inevitable that this should be attributed to the inadequacy of early childhood experiences. Dickens's other main concern in the novel is with the industrial abuses that beset society at the time. The phenomenon of industrialism as the Victorians knew it could only have happened, it is implied, because the estimate of the educability of the working people was so low. Given that they lived in a society interested only in statistical measurements, any need to consider the human and humane aspects of living was redundant.

Dickens, then, depicts the industrial environment as unlovely and threatening:

> It was a town of red brick, or of brick that would have been red if the smoke and ashes had allowed it; but, as matters stood it was a town of unnatural red and black like the painted face of a savage. (p.65)

He never tires of repeating such descriptions and finally condemns the abuses of industrialism in the words of the dying Stephen:

> I ha' fell into a pit that ha' been wi' the' Fire-damp crueller than battle. I ha' read on't in the public petition, as onny one may read, fro' the men that works in pits, in which they ha' pray'n an pray'n the lawmakers for Christ's sake not to let their work be murder to 'em. (p.290)

However much Dickens may have marred his effect by such exaggeration—as in Bounderby or indeed in Stephen Blackpool himself—the condemnation of the industrial ravages on man and nature is undeniably severe.

Some critics are of the mind that Dickens does not go far enough in his condemnation of a moral climate that would tolerate such a denial of human rights and feelings. It is claimed that he finds it easier to concentrate on ridiculing individuals and doing so in a manner which reduces them to caricatures. However, this focus on individual characters may be interpreted as part of his theme of sowing seeds and reaping the results. Victorian readers here, no doubt, appreciated the underlying New Testament adage that 'by their fruits ye shall know them' (Matthew 7.20). If Bounderby, Mrs Sparsit and Harthouse were examples of what industrial society produced, then that was a sufficiently powerful condemnation of the system.

Characterisation

Mention has been made more than once in these Notes of the term 'caricature'. In literary terms caricature means that particular features, of either appearance or habit, are described in an exaggerated manner. Dickens is often accused of using this device to excess. He is charged with drawing cartoon figures in an attempt to amuse and entertain without due reference to artistic intentions of a higher order. Thus in *Hard Times* his constant harping upon Bounderby's boasts about the way in which he was brought up, or on Mrs Sparsit's mittens, or on Bitzer's colourless appearance would all be evidences of such tendencies to caricature, while Mr Sleary's lisp and Gradgrind's square appearance would provide further examples of caricaturing effects. One critic of the art of the novel, E.M. Forster (1879–1970), has described this effect as 'flat'—by which he means to suggest that the figures are of single dimension and not, as he goes on to suggest, 'rounded'. The implication is that such treatment is out of place in any novel which purports to be taken seriously. It is being suggested in such appraisals that, if the novelist wishes to persuade us that his fiction has any relevance to real life, then his people ought to be 'real' and credible. It seems a reasonable argument.

There is, of course, the counter-argument that, in 'real life' too there are people who are underdeveloped, who have never matured in outlook, who are fixed in attitudes and habits. If *Hard Times* has a message at all this surely is it: that the very inadequacy of the educational processes obtaining at the time, and the oppressive nature of the philosophy of industrialism, would produce just such automatons, such unreal figures as Bounderby. Those whom Dickens would have us see as more estimable characters do not have the same marked idiosyncrasies as his other creations. Thus, Stephen Blackpool, Rachael and Sissy are all without easily identifiable physical peculiarities. And, though they are fixed in their own ways, Dickens suggests that this happened through a maturing process they have already experienced.

We witness this maturing process in some of his characters. For example, the square Gradgrind will, in the course of the novel, lose those harsh edges and gradually become more recognisably human. Louisa, the heroine of the novel, will be subjected to and respond to similar maturing processes.

Louisa Gradgrind

She is one of the older children in the Gradgrind family, and the main plot revolves around her. Thus she is the one whom her father regards as the exemplar in his family. When, for example, he catches her and Tom stealing a peep at the circus, his reaction is 'What would your best friend say, Louisa?'. His remarks are not addressed to Tom. And, indeed, on this occasion as on others, she speaks for both the children. She defends their presence at the circus unashamedly, for she 'wanted to see what it was like'. She defends Tom against any attack by his father by declaring that she persuaded him to accompany her.

She is a precocious child. She treats the pompous Bounderby with contempt even early in the novel when he insists on a kiss from her. And, in the same episode, she amply demonstrates how dead she is to all feeling. Dead to all, that is, except her love for Tom. It is made clear in the novel that she would do anything for him. It is a measure of her moral development in the book, in fact, that she is finally courageous enough to choose truth rather than foolishly protect him. Through her Dickens exemplifies the failure of education as practised by Gradgrind to develop sensibilities and emotion. Because of this immaturity she seems an easy victim to James Harthouse. But, for all the harm that Harthouse may have done, he effects some good. It is an ironic result of his attentions that Louisa sees the relevance of emotion. Hence, when called to her mother's death-bed, she shows herself newly capable of unselfish affection:

'I want to hear of you mother; not of myself.'
'You want to hear of me, my dear? That's something new'. (p.224)

Earlier in the novel Dickens had indicated that there were possible depths to Louisa's character. She spends many quiet hours looking into the fire and imagining many things. She has the gift of 'wondering', of imagination; but, whenever this reveals itself, it is repressed by external pressures. She herself even resists any full expression of it— hence her rejection of Sissy's influence in the early stages of the novel, and her ready acceptance of Bounderby as a husband. This act is easily seen as a triumph of the cynicism and despair in her nature.

Tom Gradgrind

From the beginning of the novel, Tom is drawn as someone who will readily use people. He abuses Louisa's blind devotion in order to gain his own way. Thus he frequently encourages her to please Bounderby so that he himself can win favours from him. At another point, he uses the ingenuousness of Stephen Blackpool to help him—unwittingly—in his plans to rob Bounderby. And, of course, he is finally dependent on a whole host of characters to aid his escape from the punishment his crime merits.

Tom is not a worthy example of the educational process or of the Gradgrind philosophy. It is, indeed, his professed intention to react against the upbringing he endured:

> I mean, I'll enjoy myself a little, and go about and see something, and hear something. I'll recompense myself for the way in which I have been brought up. (p.92)

He soon falls victim to a world which he does not fully understand, and with which he cannot cope. He incurs heavy gambling debts and is forced to steal from Bounderby. That he is not a natural thief is made clear by his frightened and disturbed appearance after the robbery has been carried out. For example, in Chapter Seven of Book the Second, we are given this account of his meeting with James Harthouse:

> 'Tom, what's the matter?'
> 'Oh! Mr Harthouse,' said Tom, with a groan, 'I am hard up, and bothered out of my life . . . . I am in a horrible mess.' (p.203)

Harthouse represents the larger world of corruption that is really, despite Tom's anxiety to experience it, well beyond his measure.

His greatest humiliation is to be found at the close of the book, where he is disguised as a black servant 'in a preposterous coat'. Of course, Dickens has made his own feelings towards Tom abundantly clear in his descriptions of him as a 'whelp'. This cowering, hangdog appearance becomes a feature of his make-up:

> He had long been a down-looking young fellow, but this characteristic had so increased of late, that he never raised his eyes to any face for three seconds together. (p.232)

Dickens does report that Tom repents and is reformed during his enforced exile, but he never lives to show his face again in England.

Sissy Jupe

Sissy Jupe belongs to a long line of Dickens's heroines. They are inevitably as white as the driven snow, angels on earth. Their influence is universally benevolent. From the time Sissy appears she is identified with heavenly light: the 'ray of sunlight', we are told, irradiated Sissy'. She is subjected to various trials at the start of the novel, both at school —her first trial is bullying in the classroom, a bullying that pursues her in the shape of Bitzer even outside the classroom—and at home. Her father abandons her to her fate early in the novel, and she waits in vain for him to return, keeping safe the oils that will soothe away his pains. This role of one who soothes and cures, is to be a major one for Sissy. She brings salve to each one's soul, redeeming even the cynical James Harthouse. While he is spoken of at one point as a witch's 'familiar', that is, one who helps in the performance of black magic, she is surely a guardian angel. Tom says that she hates him (p.91) but it is impossible to believe that she could hate anyone. It is a measure of Tom's resistance to her goodness that he attributes to her his own capacity for hate. Yet, though she is almost unearthly, she is, nevertheless, seen to be in touch with the reality of everyday life. When Tom Gradgrind is incriminated by Stephen's dying words, it is Sissy who rescues him by telling him to hide with Sleary's circus. The manner in which Dickens describes this in Chapter Seven of the Third Book shows that Sissy is not afraid to deal with evil at first hand:

> Sissy, attentive to all that happened, slipped behind that wicked shadow—a sight in the horror of his face, if there had been eyes there for any sight but one—and whispered in his ear. (p.292)

Sissy's influence touches the Stephen Blackpool plot before this, for it is she who comforts Rachael whilst she waits for Stephen's return to Coketown. She thus provides another example, and there are many, of the way in which Dickens is anxious to interweave plot and personalities in *Hard Times*.

Bitzer

Bitzer is not so much a human being as a machine, an automaton, the product of a mechanical age. He answers in the classroom in a robot-like manner, and later in the novel acts not simply of his own accord but almost as though he were programmed to do so. He responds to commands much as a computer might to the message put into it. Only in the last act of the novel, where he attempts to arrest Tom, does he seem to be acting on his own initiative. Dickens seems intent on depicting Bitzer in uniformly repulsive terms; he says that 'his skin was so unwholesomely deficient in the natural tinge, that he looked as though, if he were cut, he would bleed white.' Later in the novel, our impression of him as an automaton is reinforced by Dickens's claim that 'his mind was so exactly regulated that he had no affections or passions'. This can, however, be qualified to some extent if the reader thinks of the hate of which Bitzer is so obviously capable. He directs it towards Sissy and the Gradgrinds in a demonstrably evil manner. His role as 'light porter' is worthy of attention. The Latin translation of this term is *Lucifer*, the devil's own name! It may well have been given to Bitzer to reflect the quintessential evil Dickens has created in him.

Mrs Sparsit

Through Mrs Sparsit Dickens makes one of the novel's attacks on the class-consciousness of the England of his time. Bounderby's claim to greatness is that he has as his housekeeper one who had 'family' connections. She has nothing else to recommend her but this tenuous link with the allegedly genteel Scadgers and Powler families. But such a link, or claim to a link, is enough to establish her value and worth in the world of the *nouveau riche*. Dickens is at pains to demonstrate that such a valuation is misplaced, and that she can represent insinuating evil more perhaps than any other person in the novel.

The picture of this elderly widow whose harshness and meanness of nature seem summed up in the mittens she wears, is one of Dickens's studies, too, in repulsion. She speaks, as Dickens says, in a hypocritical manner, with, to use his words, 'an affectation of humility'. She is a fitting companion to Bounderby, the 'Bully of humility', whose protestations of his humble beginnings are as hypocritical as her semblance of devotion to him.

Her severe appearance with her hooked nose and 'dense black eyebrows' is exactly expressive of her bitter moral outlook. She is an accomplice to Bounderby in his treatment of Blackpool when he asks for advice about his marriage. She is instrumental, too, on her visit to Bounderby at his country house, in helping to widen the rift between him and Louisa. And, of course, in her frenetic zeal to re-establish her position in Bounderby's household she hunts Louisa and hunts down Bounderby's mother, Mrs Pegler.

There is some threat of caricature in the depiction of Mrs Sparsit. But this is offset by her many functions in the novel. There is even a point when, after her first meeting with James Harthouse at the bank, Dickens seems to suggest that she has developed in that short while some feeling for Harthouse; she is visibly disturbed after he has gone:

> Whether it was that the heat prevented Mrs Sparsit from working, or whether it was that her hand was out, she did no work that night . . . .
> 'O, you Fool!' said Mrs Sparsit, when she was alone at her supper. Whom she meant, she did not say. (p.157)

We have the impression that she could have amorous designs on James Harthouse as much as she had designs on Bounderby before he chose Louisa.

James Harthouse

Where Dickens had a decidedly hostile attitude to Mrs Sparsit, he does not have quite so negative an approach to Harthouse. Though

Harthouse could well have been an instrument of evil towards Louisa, for example, Dickens points out that he has no 'earnest wickedness of purpose'. What he does he does as a result of sheer boredom. His maxim in life is a simple stoical one: What will be, will be.

This is repeated in connection with Harthouse many times. He has no real commitment to anything, as he confesses to Louisa:

> Mrs Bounderby... upon my honour, no.... I assure you I attach not the least importance to any opinions. The result of the varieties of boredom I have undergone, is a conviction... that any set of ideas will do just as much good as any other set. (p.162)

There is something genuinely attractive about Harthouse, both physically and in terms of his personality. This is enough to stir feelings in Mrs Sparsit. And it is apparent, too, that after the attentions he paid Louisa she began to learn the power of the affections.

He quickly wins people's confidence, for example that of Tom and Mrs Sparsit, and is pleasantly disposed towards people as long as they add to his enjoyment. He is, however, not a dreamer but a realist. In wishing to 'go in' for things he leaves nothing to chance. Having gained Gradgrind's attention in London, he is not slow in building up Coketown connections. When Sissy faces him with the reality of Louisa's position, he readily accepts the facts and takes the necessary steps. However, on departing, Harthouse has, at last, been affected by events. Having always been 'weary of everything' he now learns at least a sense of shame, a quality that reflects a growing awareness of his relationships with others, and, perhaps, of responsibility.

Rachael

Like Sissy, Rachael is another paragon of virtue. She provides for Stephen Blackpool much the same kind of support that Sissy offers to the people in her world. The two women meet only towards the end of the novel. In her anxiety about Rachael, Sissy asks if she could visit her. Rachael gives her the highest praise possible for her kind influence:

> If it hadn't been mercifully brought about, that I was to have you to speak to,... times are, when I think my mind would not have kept right. But I get hope and strength through you. (p.275)

This is the very same service that Rachael had performed for Stephen in his trials. Stephen, estranged from his wife, had fallen in love with Rachael. The moral pressures of the time made the relationship difficult—Rachael's good name is threatened by her being seen in the company of a man known to be married—but Rachael offers Stephen a sincere and lasting friendship. Her moral courage is displayed in her kindness, too, to Stephen's wife when she returns to Coketown in a drunken state. And, as the final chapter tells us, she continues these ministrations long after Stephen is dead, for Rachael cannot think evil of anyone.

In her final trial, when suspicions about Stephen's guilt seem confirmed by his failure to return to Coketown, she does find it difficult to forgive Louisa for her supposed complicity with Tom:

> The like of you don't know us, don't care for us, don't belong to us. I am not sure why you may ha' come that night. I can't tell but what you may ha' come with some aim of your own . . . . (p.270)

But later she begs to be forgiven for such thoughts as 'It goes against me . . . to mistrust anyone.' The real depths of the love she has for Stephen are never made clear to the reader until that terrible moment when she realises that he has fallen into the pit. We then witness a hysteria that could perhaps never have been anticipated in a woman with such self-control. However, it is the emotional expression of one who has, in Stephen's interests, restrained herself for so long:

> 'O, my good Lord! He's down there! Down there!' At first this, and her terrific screams, were all that could be got from Rachael . . . . It was impossible to hush her . . . . (p.284)

Many a Victorian heart at that point would, no doubt, have wished that it had been possible for Rachael to have made her feelings so eloquently known to Stephen long before that tragedy.

Mr Bounderby

Dickens condemns Bounderby from the start by his calculated description of the repulsive physical features of the man:

> A man with a great puffed head and forehead, swelled veins in his temples, and such a strained skin to his face that it seemed to hold his eyes open and lift his eyebrows up. (p.58)

This description follows immediately after the scene in which Gradgrind threatens Louisa with Bounderby's displeasure. By creating the link between Bounderby and Louisa, between Old Age and Youth, Dickens reinforces this repulsive effect. She marries him out of a sense of duty to her family and certainly not through any feelings of love.

Bounderby's self-complacency is one of his more unattractive qualities. He is assured that he is worthy of respect and esteem because he is a self-made man. It is his constant boast that he has made his way in the world and achieved success without the help of anyone. He sees himself, too, as a benefactor to his employees. These two features are given expression in his first conversation with Harthouse:

> I'll state the fact of it to you. It's the pleasantest work there is, and it's the lightest work there is, and it's the best paid work there is . . . . So now, we may shake hands on equal terms. I say, equal terms, because although I know what I am, and the exact depth of the gutter I have lifted myself out of . . . I am as proud as you are . . . .
> (pp.159–60)

Of course, the inaccuracy of the first part of what he says is blatantly clear, and the untruth of the second is dramatically revealed later in the novel when his mother is brought upon the scene.

There is not a single redeeming feature in Bounderby's character. He is, as Dickens frequently describes him, a 'Bully'. None of the goodness in the novel ever moves him. Even the presence of both Sissy and Rachael has no effect on him. Dickens does appear to bring him low by his mother's revelations, but we are bound to believe that, with his customary 'inflation', he will rise above even that.

He is, however, to be humiliated at the moment of his death, for he dies ignominiously in a fit in a street. He had hoped to make sure through his will that his name would always be honoured, but Dickens tells us that the law—for which Bounderby claimed to have much admiration—would effectively turn this plan into an unrealised dream.

Mr Gradgrind

When reading Dickens we are always looking for some significance in the names he give his characters. We might, for example, like to conjecture that Bounderby is so named because he is by nature a bounder, a cheat, a deceiver who seeks advancement at the expense of others. In fact, 'Bounder' was Dickens original name for him! No name, however, seems to reward our attention so much in *Hard Times* as that of Gradgrind, with all its connotations of slavish attention to petty detail—the 'grind'—and its concern with the different stages of our lives—the 'grade' or 'grad'. Because of his insistence that his children should attend to factual matters alone they are in danger of never developing fully as people.

Gradgrind's name, however, proves a certain disservice to him in the novel. In the first place, it must not be forgotten that it was he who had offered Sissy Jupe a home. And this action was very much against the advice and wish of Bounderby, who saw in it a threat to Louisa and Tom. And indeed, this action does have a profound effect on Louisa, and on the other members of the Gradgrind family.

In many ways, Dickens is sympathetic towards Gradgrind. He never attributes ill-will to him—he never hurts anyone intentionally. Louisa, whom we may well regard as a victim of her father, assures him 'I have never blamed you and I never shall.' But there is some ambivalence in Dickens's depiction of Gradgrind. For, having observed in the beginning of Book Three a distinct change of heart in Gradgrind, we then find him, in Chapter Five of the same book, reverting to what he had been: dictatorial, giving his full support to Bounderby. Our unfavourable impression of him in this one episode, however, is fully offset by his later forgiving attitude towards Tom, and his wish to help him to escape punishment. That, indeed, is a change from the Gradgrind who would have penalised his children for stealing a peep at a circus.

Stephen Blackpool

The most damning comment on Stephen is made by James Harthouse in Chapter Ten of Book Two. In conversation with Louisa, he speaks of him as 'an infinitely dreary person .... Lengthy and prosy in the extreme'. The description is not inappropriate. Though Dickens tells us that Stephen's own assessment of his situation was that he had only 'a peck of trouble' the impression he conveys with monotonous regularity in the novel is one of carrying a dreadful weight of sorrow. Of course, a reader is bound to sympathise with 'Old Stephen'—but he does test our tolerance. He never appears without conveying the impression that life is a burden.

Stephen is dogged, first of all, by the mistake of his marriage to a woman who has taken to drink, been unfaithful to him, and abandoned him. He tries to build up a new life, but she keeps returning, selling his belongings to get money for more drink, and leaving him again in further despair. He then falls foul of his fellow-workers for refusing to join the union. But this, far from recommending him to his employer, actually precipitates his dismissal. He cannot even leave the town without unwittingly setting up a hue and cry!

Stephen is his own worst enemy; he confides in people who are obviously unsympathetic to him. It was, for example, utterly foolish of him to confide in Bounderby in such express terms about his marriage. This lack of insight into other people's characters is made evident again when he agrees so readily to Tom Gradgrind's request that he loiter about the bank for three nights. Only on the third night did he begin 'to have an uncomfortable sensation' that he might be incurring suspicion! Stephen, in other words, seems ill-equipped to deal with the world. He even botches his return to Coketown to redeem his name. We might be forgiven for thinking that it was singularly appropriate that Stephen should choose to travel at night in a notoriously dangerous area.

All of this may appear a harsh assessment of a character whom Dickens is obviusly using to stir up our pity and emotion. It may be, however, that Dickens tried too hard to encourage his readers to accept such a catalogue of woes. Stephen's constant complaint that it is 'aw a muddle' may be designed to pluck at our heart strings, but it can have an equally negative effect in highlighting the character's ineptitude in dealing with real life. His death scene causes problems in our understanding of his character. The author insists that what he says is expressed 'without anger against anyone', but Stephen's words at that point seem embittered and despairing. It is claimed that he makes no accusation against Tom and that he is only intent on clearing his own name. But he confesses that he had indeed been angry with both Louisa and Tom until the time of quiet reflection which he had been forced to pass in the pit alleviated his anger somewhat. But even as he dies, he points an accusing finger at Tom.

It may be argued that Dickens chose Stephen as an example of the injury industry can do to man. Indeed, as he dies, Blackpool sighs:

> I ha' read on't in the public petition, as onny one may read, fro' the men that works in pits, in which they ha' pray'n an pray'n the law-makers for Christ's sake not to let their work be murder to 'em, but to spare 'em for th' wives and children . . . . (p.290)

It seems unfortunate, nevertheless, that Dickens chose as his so-called champion of the workers' rights one so obviously ill-equipped to deal with his own problems. When given the opportunity to defend his decision not to join the union, Stephen fails to produce anything but an appeal for pity. It cannot be said that he based his feelings on principle. He does indeed claim that he doubted that joining a union would do anybody any good, but that is scarcely a very cogent response. The fact is he did what he did in fulfilment of a promise to Rachael; but, admirable as Rachael is, Stephen's decision is not easily defended by reference to her sound judgement.

Mrs Pegler and Mrs Gradgrind

The function of these two ladies is obviously not central to the novel. Mrs Gradgrind is useful initially in providing support in the Gradgrind household for its master's philosophy. But otherwise she is so enfeebled by illness throughout the novel that she can hardly be called an active participant. She does, however, make her greatest contribution to the novel as she dies. For then she persuades Louisa to pay heed to Sissy's benevolent influence and to the lessons she can offer in goodness.

Mrs Pegler, for her part, is simply used in the novel to provide a measure of the depths to which Bounderby is prepared to plunge. He is constantly denouncing his mother for having neglected him as a child and using this alleged neglect to demonstrate how well he has fared despite initial set-backs. Mrs Pegler is eventually given the opportunity to show that these allegations are wickedly untrue.

Her occasional unheralded appearances through the novel are used to add more mystery, to rouse even more curiosity in the reader. But, besides this, these appearances are shrewdly used by the author to lend credibility to the charge laid against her later of complicity in the bank robbery. Thus Mrs Pegler contributes to the structure of the novel and plays a clearly defined part in the plot.

The style of *Hard Times*

The opening paragraphs of the novel provide many instances of one significant feature of Dickens's style, namely, his love of repetition. He likes, for example, to sample single words: the word 'Fact' is singled out and re-introduced over and over again.

He is fond, too, of the use of repetition for rhetorical effect, and this is exemplified in the reiteration of the same opening of sentences in paragraph two of the novel: 'The emphasis was'. This is not a very subtle stylistic device but its insistent obviousness accords well with the squareness and bluntness of Gradgrind's appearance as described in this opening scene.

Dickens likes to introduce any striking details very quickly. Thus Gradgrind is square, Bitzer light, Bounderby round. These features, once introduced, are there for good. Indeed, Dickens takes obvious delight in ringing the changes on such features by piling detail on similar detail:

> Thomas Gradgrind, sir. A man of realities. A man of fact and calculations. A man who proceeds upon the principle that two and two are four, and nothing over, and who is not to be talked into allowing for anything over. Thomas Gradgrind, sir—peremptorily Thomas—Thomas Gradgrind. (p.48)

Dickens employs this stylistic trick not in descriptions of people alone. Detail on detail is the device he uses, for example, in his depiction of Coketown:

> It was a town of red brick, or of brick that would have been red if the smoke and ashes had allowed it; but, as matters stood it was a town of unnatural red and black like the painted face of a savage. It was a town of machinery and tall chimneys, out of which interminable serpents of smoke trailed themselves for ever and ever . . . . (p.65)

Irony

The grim reality of the town is ironically treated. That end phrase 'for ever and ever' has a fairy-story ring to it; it is almost as if Dickens were describing gleaming fairy palaces. Such irony is a further device in his repertoire. It may take the form of ironic coincidence, as evidenced, say, in the fact that Stephen and Mrs Pegler—both 'watchers' outside the bank—come to be charged as accomplices. Or it may be the grim irony shown in Tom Gradgrind's eventual dressing up as a clown in the final scenes of the novel in complete contradistinction to the ambitions his father had for him. Or it may be the total irony of Bounderby's eventual disgrace through the revelation of the truth about his childhood.

Irony is not the only evidence of Dickensian humour even in *Hard Times*. The novel may lack that sense of boisterous good humour that is a feature of many of his other books. But simple humour for its own sake is still to be found, for example, in his descriptions of people. Thus his accounts of various stages of baldness in Gradgrind and Bounderby show the author in full enjoyment of his own inventiveness:

> The emphasis was helped by the speaker's hair, which bristled on the skirts of his bald head, a plantation of firs to keep the wind from its shining surface, all covered with knobs, like the crust of a plum pie. (p.47)

This is his description of Gradgrind's head. The description of Bounderby is not dissimilar:

> He had not much hair. One might have fancied he had talked it off; and that what was left, all standing up in disorder, was in that condition from being blown about by his windy boastfulness. (p.59)

These descriptions illustrate Dickens's sense of the ridiculous, a feature again exemplified in his description of Mrs Sparsit's relation, Lady Scadgers—'an immensely fat old woman, with an inordinate appetite for butcher's meat, and a mysterious leg which had now refused to get out of bed for fourteen years.'

Dickens is not, however, simply pleased to entertain himself. Occasionally he likes to show someone else gaining enjoyment out of such a facetious approach to life. Thus, James Harthouse—whilst not the most estimable of characters—is used to poke fun at other, grosser people. For example, when Mrs Sparsit attempts to be philosophical and gives voice to the banality 'We live in a singular world, sir', Harthouse comments in eloquent terms:

> I have had the honour, by a coincidence of which I am proud, to have made a remark, similar in effect, though not so epigrammatically expressed. (p.219)

Mr M'Choakumchild – specific satire. Part I Chap 2.

The tone is most appropriate in its devastating mockery of Mrs Sparsit
—an effect enjoyed by the reader but quite lost on Mrs Sparsit!
Dickens never tires of poking fun at her. The scene in which, above all,
he seems to be enjoying the fun himself is that in which she spies on
Louisa and Harthouse. There, Dickens's technique of accumulation of
detail destroys any sense of dignity Mrs Sparsit had ever intended to
convey:

> Wet through and through: with her feet squelching and squashing in
> her shoes whenever she moved; with a rash of rain upon her classical
> visage; with a bonnet like an over-ripe fig; with all her clothes
> spoiled; with damp impressions of every button, string, and hook-
> and-eye she wore, printed off upon her highly-connected back; with
> a stagnant verdure on her general exterior, such as accumulates on
> an old park fence in a mouldy lane. (p.238)

It may be that Dickens's humour becomes somewhat 'caustic', a word
used by Harthouse to describe Tom Gradgrind. His description of
members of Parliament as 'the national dustmen' could stand as a
further simple example of this. But at times his humour is gentle and
mild. The lisp he gives Sleary provides an example of this: it can be seen
as poking fun rather cruelly, but it is more fruitful to see it as evidence
of his wish to show a childlike innocence and sincerity that are too
often lacking in other people in the novel.

Part 4

Hints for study

THE FIRST THING is to read the novel through completely. These Notes can in no way substitute for the need to experience Dickens at first-hand. Read *Hard Times* for enjoyment. It has plenty of that to offer. Do not see it as some kind of imposition. Try to make its many characters come to life for you; try to enter their world.

Once having sampled the flavour, you can begin to bite into and digest the dish more slowly. You might set about making your own summaries and commentaries on each chapter as you make your way through the novel on a second reading. At each point, that is, at the end of each chapter, compare your version with that offered in this book. This double process will help you to fix the narrative in your mind and also to formulate opinions about characters, themes, and so on.

Having established certain attitudes towards the text, you ought to read Part 3 of the Notes to see how far it agrees with your own impressions, provides new ideas and, indeed, omits points of view which you have established to your own personal satisfaction.

Do not read Part 3, the Critical Commentary, passively. Adopt a critical perspective yourself—not carping or negative but positive and constructive, by looking for further substantiation and justification of the various points made there. You should notice an insistence on textual evidence in the Commentary. For, in your examination, you will need to demonstrate such a willingness to make close references to the text of the novel.

Quotations

Lengthy, verbatim quotations from prose works are not expected of you in examinations. It is generally recognised that the learning of lengthy prose quotations is not only demanding in simple memory terms but also wasteful of valuable time and energies better expended in a more constructive and creative manner. So do not learn by heart quotations of any great length. Short phrases which capture the essential Dickensian flavour can be both manageable for you and well received by your examiner. So, Dickens's references to, say, Gradgrind's 'square wall of forehead', or Coketown's 'river that ran purple with ill-smelling dye' or the 'melancholy madness' of the steam-engine are examples of phrases that, punctuating your own statements, would show that you have a good grasp of Dickens's prose.

Of course, as you write your preparatory essays on the text, you will necessarily wish to extract sentences to prove your points. It is, however, a different matter to have the text before you for consultation and to be without it in an examination room.

In looking at the questions and answers which follow here, make sure that you avoid mere passive review. Instead, you should try to answer the questions yourself first of all and then compare what you have written with the response given in these Notes. This procedure of self-testing is much more fruitful than passive acceptance of views offered.

Planning an answer

The first step in planning an answer is to look carefully at the question to which such an answer will purport to offer a reply. Under examination conditions where you may well feel tense and anxious, the wording of the question can prove a life-line—something to hang on to until you get your breath. Take care to notice the clues offered by the question in order to approach it sensibly.

Relevance must be your first consideration. At all costs avoid straying into irrelevancies. Candidates do, at times, feel the need to try to impress the examiner by including material of various kinds. Unless this material can be presented as relevant to the question as it is set, omit it.

A further point: do not attempt to shape a previous answer you may have provided on *Hard Times* to 'fit' a question in the paper. Look at each question as a fresh challenge. You will then handle it in a 'fresh' way. It happens very rarely indeed that the wording of a question you have previously attempted will coincide with that in the examination paper. Preparing your examination answer may be usefully done by clearly defined stages. These are best exemplified by the study of a particular question. Let us suppose that the following statement was set for your consideration: 'The evils which he attacks he caricatures grossly, and with little humour.' You might handle this in the following manner:

Stage 1: Break down the statement into its component parts thus: The evils which he attacks/he caricatures/grossly/and with little humour.

Stage 2: Make an outline noting possible material for each part, thus:

evils: greed, poverty, inhumanity, hypocrisy, environmental conditions, education *caricatures*: consideration of Dickens's style—exaggeration, typification, focus on the odd and the eccentric

grossly: is this accurate? how acceptable in particular instances? how unacceptable?

little humour: recognition of some truth in this—some qualification though

Stage 3: Search for evidence in each of the parts of Stage 2

Stage 4: General assessment of an appropriate perspective to adopt in the light of the original statement

Below, in the section 'Specimen answers', you will find an answer to this question offered in fully worked-out form based on the plan outlined here. Try it yourself first, though.

Specimen answers

1. 'The evils which he attacks he caricatures grossly, and with little humour.' Discuss this assessment of Dickens's social criticism in *Hard Times*.

The prevalence of evil is undoubted in the world with which Dickens deals in *Hard Times*. The opening pages expose the evil of the educational philosophy to which the children are subjected, an education allowing no access to the world of wonder or imagination but insisting instead on pragmatic proof and evidence.

Dickens's technique in his attack on this attitude toward child education is to associate the ugly with the empirical search for facts, and the beautiful with the search for 'fancy'. Thus Gradgrind, the owner of the model school, is characterised as formidable and forbidding with a 'square wall of forehead'. Bitzer, the star pupil, has what to Dickens are repulsively lifeless features, and looks as if 'he would bleed white' if he were cut.

The champion of the imaginative, on the other hand, is associated with beauty. Sissy Jupes is pretty and a heavenly light shines on her. Moreover, she speaks of a world and an environment which are attractive, human and welcoming. That such a spirit should be threatened by the malignant forces marshalled against it is itself sufficient evidence of how bitterly opposed Dickens is to the Hard Facts men in education.

Dickens focuses his attention on this evil throughout the book, not only in its opening chapters. His titles for each of the separate Books constituting *Hard Times* demonstrate his insistent concern with the nature of education. They suggest that those who sow evil seeds at the early stage will reap their due pernicious reward later.

This particular evil, of the wanton destruction of the mind, is closely related to the evil of the industrial ravaging of England through the irresponsible actions of profiteers and entrepreneurs. The grim picture of Coketown with its sulphurous air and the 'serpents of smoke' is one that is repeated almost *ad nauseam* by the author. In appearance Coketown is of 'unnatural red and black like the painted face of a savage'. That Bounderby should later boast to James Harthouse that the lethal smoke is 'the healthiest thing in the world' is a part of Dickens's caustic attack on this evil.

The fact is, of course, that Bounderby thrives on the smoke himself, in the sense that he gets rich from its proceeds. But Dickens points out that he is quick to put fifteen miles between himself and Coketown when he gets married. He does so on the back, as it were, of a bankrupt who had lost all his property. Bounderby quickly avails himself of opportunities to benefit by others' misfortunes. The malaise of poverty is sharply contrasted with the wealth which Bounderby enjoys. Stephen Blackpool's poverty, for example, is nowhere so clearly shown than in the scene where he approaches Bounderby for advice about his marriage. There we are told that Stephen snatches a quick bite of 'but a little bread' while his employer enjoys sherry and chops.

This division between wealth and poverty is emphasised by Bounderby's remarks that the workers have ambitions above their station in life—they expect, as he puts it, to feed off 'turtle soup and venison'. The inhumanity which Bounderby shows towards Stephen and his fellow-workers is but one instance of something that Dickens sees as a pervasive attitude in the society he depicts. His attacks on laws which are inhumane, his presentation of the indifference that members of Parliament, 'the national dustmen', show to the public interest, his portrayal of the vindictive nature of some of his characters all serve to show that man's inhumanity to man is everywhere evident. This is what led Chesterton to describe *Hard Times* as 'the harshest of his stories'.

This comment suggests that Chesterton takes Dickens's charges and his treatment of the theme seriously. The comment under consideration in this essay questions the serious effect of Dickens's novel in its charge that what Dickens offers is a 'caricature' of reality. By this, it would seem that the critic is stressing Dickens's tendency to exaggeration which threatens to be ridiculous. The further charge that he does this 'grossly' is damning in the extreme.

That Dickens does employ caricature as a technique is generally allowed. The figure of Bounderby, for example, is obviously one that is a composite of many people. Dickens has rolled (and in Bounderby's case a sense of rolling rotundity is inevitable) many people into one. The result is obvious exaggeration. But such exaggeration as exists serves an artistic purpose. The large, pompous Bounderby who seems 'inflated like a balloon' is Dickens's picture of the self-made man of industry. It is apt that the 'Bully of humility' should constantly do violence to that virtue in his hypocritical accounts of his lowly origins. The perhaps cumbersome repetition of these falsehoods exactly parallels the incessant movement of his machines in 'a state of melancholy madness'. We should be foolish to look for finesse in Bounderby just as we should look in vain for elegance in his elephantine machines.

But though such a figure as Bounderby may be 'gross' it can hardly be claimed with justice that Dickens handles his depiction 'grossly'; he is of a piece with the world he represents. He is given his proper place in the novel, making his decisions in matters both mechanical and moral and, like others in the novel, reaping his due reward!

Dickens is constantly aware of the danger of creating too doleful a picture and of thereby becoming indeed 'gross' in his method and effects. But we can find plenty of instances where even the ugly is offset by Dickens's humorous touches. For example, when describing Stone Lodge, Gradgrind's house, he gives each specific detail of its structure even to the evidence of its 'iron clamps and girders'—not a single attractive, picturesque detail in the whole lengthy list of features. But he then brings the whole thing crashing down with impish delight with the single phrase: 'everything that heart could desire'.

Dickens revels, of course, in comic description. This is clearly shown in the characters attached to the circus—the contrasting figures of E.W.B. Childers and Master Kidderminster, for example, or the lisping Sleary 'with one fixed eye and one loose eye'. Dickens is obviously enjoying himself among these circus performers, and the episodes involving them would have us call in question the charge of 'little humour' referred to in the essay title. The lightness of touch we experience there is not absent either in his dealings with the more serious characters. The descriptions of Bounderby's and Gradgrind's baldness are a ready example of Dickens's willingness to play with details with the same whimsicality as he imagines the wind plays with their wisps of hair.

Instances could be multiplied, but enough has probably been said here to show that *Hard Times* has plenty of humour. Despite Dickens's preoccupation with the mechanical in *Hard Times*, a theme that might well be described as gross, it is not true to dismiss his treatment of this and other themes as gross caricature. There is, indeed, caricature, but even in such an extreme case as that of Bounderby, the artist is clearly at work.

COMMENTARY: This approach to the essay has been favourable to Dickens throughout. What *you* wrote in your answer may have been in support of the critic's sentiments. As long as you are able to provide textual substantiation your own approach is as valid as that above.

2. 'Of all Dickens' works it is the one that has all the strength of his genius together with a strength no other of them can show—that of a completely serious work of art.' Discuss F.R. Leavis's assessment of *Hard Times*.

To handle the question comprehensively would necessitate as investigation of the rest of Dickens's works, which would be a formidable task indeed! Given the constraints of time and space we must test the validity of the praise here accorded to *Hard Times* by consideration of that novel alone.

The 'strength of his genius' in *Hard Times* is tested in the characters he creates. Dickens's characters, it is often claimed, run the risk of being relegated to the level of caricature. If this were indeed the case in *Hard Times* then the description of the novel as a 'completely serious work of art' would seem inappropriate. For the existence of caricature argues that a less than serious intention is in evidence—at least in part.

If caricature were to exist at all in the novel then this would certainly leave open to question the absolute nature of the claim made by Leavis. It seems unfortunate that Leavis did not here wish to qualify his assertion, for the opening chapters of the novel do abound in what appear to be caricatures. The figures of Gradgrind, M'Choakumchild, Bitzer and Bounderby are all capable of being interpreted in this way. The absolute squareness of Gradgrind, the inflated rotundity of Bounderby set them in this mould. This delight in typification is in evidence in the later stages of the novel, too, in such figures as Harthouse, the typical 'cad', or Mrs Sparsit, the mittened Medusa of *Hard Times*!

It would, however, be unjust to dismiss Dickens's characterisation in this novel as simply indulging in caricature, for he is obviously at pains to demonstrate growth and development in some at least of his central figures. That they can grow and mature is evidence of a more serious artistic commitment by the novelist. We find it, indeed, even in such an initially unpromising figure as Gradgrind. The square, rough edges of his character are gradually smoothed by his harrowing experiences later in the novel. There is evidence of it also in the depiction of Louisa, who resists the influence of good for a long time but yields to it eventually.

Unfortunately, it is not a consistently successful artistic device in the novel. Tom Gradgrind, for example, only comes to the light, as it were, in Dickens's epilogue (he calls it 'Final') to the novel; this is a comparatively crude technique of showing development outside the boundaries proper of the work.

That he should make such efforts at serious depiction, however, does argue for seriousness of artistic intent. The development of these various characters is, indeed, of a piece with one of the central concerns in his book, namely, the dangers to personal development in the individual, resulting from misguided and inadequate educational philosophies. Thus the emphasis on facts to the disadvantage of the development of the imagination is shown by Dickens to threaten further development in the individual.

This is a theme of very serious intent in the novel and one that prompts the author to insist that we pay attention to it. He does so, however, by presenting us with extremes: the evidence of the absolutely good and the absolutely bad. Sissy Jupe is presented as the epitome of goodness, Bitzer as that of evil. there is no doubt that such is his intention. There is, indeed, more than a suggestion of exaggeration in his presentation, and we are therefore bound to question whether this is in accord with the valuation of the novel as a 'serious work of art.'

One strength that Dickens does reveal in *Hard Times*, which might have earned Leavis's approval, is the careful construction of plots. There are two plots in the novel, one involving the Gradgrind family and the other involving Stephen Blackpool. There was indeed a danger that the latter could simply have become a sentimental melodrama. To make Stephen suffer would have brought delighted tears of sympathy to the readers' eyes. But Dickens resisted the temptation simply to exploit the Blackpool plot emotionally and instead knitted it skilfully and artistically into the Gradgrind pattern. He did this by having them share a thematic interest: the role of the individual in an industrial society, and by having characters slip quite naturally from one plot to the other. Herein lies the novel's strongest claim to be regarded as a 'completely serious work of art'. Ironically, its clarity and coherence are in sharp contrast to Stephen Blackpool's assertion about his world, namely, that it is 'aw a muddle'!

COMMENTARY: Here relevance is maintained by constant reference to the original statement made in the essay title. This is a useful device for demonstrating to the examiner that you are concerned with the relevance of your answer to the terms of the question.

3. What is the part played by Sissy Jupe in *Hard Times*?

The part played by Sissy Jupe seems obvious from the start of the novel: to provide a clear-cut contrast to the experiences of those caught up in purely functional education. Thus she is shown in Chapter One to be at odds with the instruction meted out to the hordes of children in Gradgrind's classroom. Dickens shows her as being, literally, at the other end of the spectrum. For the light that catches her at 'the beginning of a sunbeam' touches Bitzer only weakly at the other end. Her natural resistance to the laws of Fact persists even when she is a member of Gradgrind's household. Sissy is thus to be seen as Dickens's example of one educated in the school of life rather than in the artificially created atmosphere of the schoolroom.

This is a romantic notion shown in sharp relief against a backcloth of harsh industrialisation. Sissy, in fact, never touches the grosser elements in life until later in the novel. It is strange, considering her impact on the Gradgrind family, that she actually fades into the background for much of the central part of the novel. Yet, though Sissy does 'disappear', Dickens makes it clear that she has been a persistently benign influence. On her return to his pages it is shown that she has been effective in the mellowing of both Gradgrind parents. And when Louisa meets her sister Jane in Book Three and comments on her 'beaming face', Jane attributes it to Sissy when she says 'I am sure it must be Sissy's doing.'

Sissy's insistent kindness is a device which facilitates the knitting together of the Gradgrind plot and that of Stephen Blackpool. For Sissy befriends Rachael and is instrumental in the final discovery of Stephen. This is the first offer of help, incidentally, that Stephen and Rachael had ever received, and it is to be contrasted with the harsh refusal to help by the industrialist Bounderby.

Bounderby had originally warned Gradgrind against the dangers of Sissy's influence. Nevertheless, Gradgrind had agreed that Sissy should live in his family and this humanitarian act was indeed the beginning of a dramatic change in Gradgrind. With all these positive notions in mind, though, there is a certain ambivalence in Sissy's role. The stress has been so far on Sissy as a symbol of wholesomeness. In this respect, commentators on the novel are happy to try to show that this healthy aspect is connected with the world of the imagination and balance as represented by the circus. This latter quality of balance has even been said to be epitomised in the human pyramid described in the opening book as one of the acts in the circus.

It ought not to be forgotten, though, that Sissy's father does abandon his child, and take with him another object of her affections, Merrylegs. It can be argued with some force here that the incident is as much an evidence of family division as the human pyramid is of interdependence, and that, within the world of fancy, the ugly side of life can also be evident.

Sissy's experience of such grim reality as the loss of a father may well be seen as having equipped her for dealing with other harsh features in life. It may, for example, be useful in helping to make more credible her influence over James Harthouse. His change of heart—if indeed he had a heart—was brought about by Sissy in a manner which could put our credulity to the test. If, however, we see it in the light of Sissy's emotional maturity, it may well be judged as artistically appropriate.

Sissy's part is summed up in Dickens's epilogue to the novel where he speaks of her continuing in later life 'to know her humbler fellow-creatures, and to beautify their lives of machinery and reality with those imaginative graces and delights, without which the heart of infancy will wither up.'

Some further questions on *Hard Times*

1. 'The story is flat and unprofitable; a mere dull melodrama in which character is caricature, sentiment tinsel, and moral (if any) unsound'. Discuss this view of *Hard Times*.
2. Show how Dickens deflates the self-importance of Bounderby, Harthouse and Mrs Sparsit.
3. Examine the comedy in *Hard Times*.
4. Examine in detail the chapter 'Men and Brothers' and show what we learn there about (i) Slackbridge, (ii) Stephen Blackpool. What is the importance of this incident in the novel as a whole?
5. 'Scheming and plotting are essential elements in story of *Hard Times*.' How true have your found this to be?
6. From your reading of *Hard Times* write an assessment of Dickens's views on marriage.
7. Give a brief physical description of each of the major characters in the novel. What have you learned from these descriptions of Dickens's descriptive technique?
8. Identify each of the circus people and make brief notes on what each contributes to your understanding of the novel.
9. How well does the title *Hard Times* suit Dickens's tale?
10. In what various ways does Dickens establish a sense of unity and coherence in his novel?

Part 5

Suggestions for further reading

The text

The edition of *Hard Times* used in the preparation of these Notes is that published by Penguin, Harmondsworth, 1969, in the Penguin English Library series. This text follows that originally published by Bradbury & Evans, London, 1854.

Criticism and Biography

BUTT, JOHN, AND TILLOTSON, KATHLEEN: *Dickens at Work*, Methuen, London, 1957. Chapters 1 and 8 deal with Dickens's writing of serials and of *Hard Times* respectively.

COLLINS, PHILIP (ED.): *Dickens, the Critical Heritage*, Routledge and Kegan Paul, London, 1971. Pages 300−53 are of particular interest to readers of *Hard Times*. A variety of opinions about the novel printed over the years is offered here.

FORD, G.H., AND LANE, L. (EDS): *The Dickens Critics*, Cornell University Press, Ithaca, New York, 1961. Useful stimulus for thinking about Dickens's novel.

GROSS, JOHN, AND PEARSON, GABRIEL (EDS): *Dickens and the Twentieth Century*, Routledge and Kegan Paul, London, 1962. See, particularly, the chapter by John Holloway on *Hard Times*.

LEAVIS, F.R., AND LEAVIS, Q.,: *Dickens the Novelist*, Penguin Books, Harmondsworth, 1970. There is a chapter here, again, dedicated to *Hard Times*.

PRICE, M, (ED.): *Dickens: A Collection of Critical Essays*, Prentice-Hall, Englewood Cliffs, New Jersey, 1973. This book is published in the 'Twentieth Century Views' series.

WILSON, ANGUS: *The World of Charles Dickens*, Secker and Warburg, London, 1970. A delightful, well-illustrated book which provides very readable background information to Dickens.

The author of these notes

DOMINIC HYLAND was educated at the Universities of Cambridge, Manchester and Lancaster. He has taught English in schools, Colleges and Polytechnics, as well as with the Universities of Liverpool, Lancaster and the Open University. He has examined English Literature at Ordinary and Advanced Levels for the G.C.E., and is currently Chief Examiner in English Literature with one of the largest Examining Boards in the country. He has written five York Notes as well as a variety of other Study Aids in Literature and English Language.

York Notes: list of titles

HENRY FIELDING
Joseph Andrews
Tom Jones

F. SCOTT FITZGERALD
Tender is the Night
The Great Gatsby

GUSTAVE FLAUBERT
Madame Bovary

E. M. FORSTER
A Passage to India
Howards End

JOHN FOWLES
The French Lieutenant's Woman

JOHN GALSWORTHY
Strife

MRS GASKELL
North and South

WILLIAM GOLDING
Lord of the Flies
The Spire

OLIVER GOLDSMITH
She Stoops to Conquer
The Vicar of Wakefield

ROBERT GRAVES
Goodbye to All That

GRAHAM GREENE
Brighton Rock
The Heart of the Matter
The Power and the Glory

WILLIS HALL
The Long and the Short and the Tall

THOMAS HARDY
Far from the Madding Crowd
Jude the Obscure
Selected Poems
Tess of the D'Urbervilles
The Mayor of Casterbridge
The Return of the Native
The Woodlanders

L. P. HARTLEY
The Go-Between

NATHANIEL HAWTHORNE
The Scarlet Letter

SEAMUS HEANEY
Selected Poems

ERNEST HEMINGWAY
A Farewell to Arms
The Old Man and the Sea

SUSAN HILL
I'm the King of the Castle

BARRY HINES
Kes

HOMER
The Iliad
The Odyssey

GERARD MANLEY HOPKINS
Selected Poems

TED HUGHES
Selected Poems

ALDOUS HUXLEY
Brave New World

HENRIK IBSEN
A Doll's House

HENRY JAMES
The Portrait of a Lady
Washington Square

BEN JONSON
The Alchemist
Volpone

JAMES JOYCE
A Portrait of the Artist as a Young Man
Dubliners

JOHN KEATS
Selected Poems

PHILIP LARKIN
Selected Poems

D. H. LAWRENCE
Selected Short Stories
Sons and Lovers
The Rainbow
Women in Love

HARPER LEE
To Kill a Mocking-Bird

LAURIE LEE
Cider with Rosie

CHRISTOPHER MARLOWE
Doctor Faustus

HERMAN MELVILLE
Moby Dick

THOMAS MIDDLETON *and*
    WILLIAM ROWLEY
The Changeling

ARTHUR MILLER
A View from the Bridge
Death of a Salesman
The Crucible

JOHN MILTON
Paradise Lost I & II
Paradise Lost IV & IX
Selected Poems

V. S. NAIPAUL
A House for Mr Biswas

ROBERT O'BRIEN
Z for Zachariah

SEAN O'CASEY
Juno and the Paycock

GEORGE ORWELL
Animal Farm
Nineteen Eighty-four

JOHN OSBORNE
Look Back in Anger
WILFRED OWEN
Selected Poems
ALAN PATON
Cry, The Beloved Country
THOMAS LOVE PEACOCK
Nightmare Abbey and *Crotchet Castle*
HAROLD PINTER
The Caretaker
SYLVIA PLATH
Selected Works
PLATO
The Republic
ALEXANDER POPE
Selected Poems
J. B. PRIESTLEY
An Inspector Calls
WILLIAM SHAKESPEARE
A Midsummer Night's Dream
Antony and Cleopatra
As You Like It
Coriolanus
Hamlet
Henry IV Part I
Henry IV Part II
Henry V
Julius Caesar
King Lear
Macbeth
Measure for Measure
Much Ado About Nothing
Othello
Richard II
Richard III
Romeo and Juliet
Sonnets
The Merchant of Venice
The Taming of the Shrew
The Tempest
The Winter's Tale
Troilus and Cressida
Twelfth Night
GEORGE BERNARD SHAW
Arms and the Man
Candida
Pygmalion
Saint Joan
The Devil's Disciple
MARY SHELLEY
Frankenstein
PERCY BYSSHE SHELLEY
Selected Poems
RICHARD BRINSLEY SHERIDAN
The Rivals

R. C. SHERRIFF
Journey's End
JOHN STEINBECK
Of Mice and Men
The Grapes of Wrath
The Pearl
LAURENCE STERNE
A Sentimental Journey
Tristram Shandy
TOM STOPPARD
Professional Foul
Rosencrantz and Guildenstern are Dead
JONATHAN SWIFT
Gulliver's Travels
JOHN MILLINGTON SYNGE
The Playboy of the Western World
TENNYSON
Selected Poems
W. M. THACKERAY
Vanity Fair
J. R. R. TOLKIEN
The Hobbit
MARK TWAIN
Huckleberry Finn
Tom Sawyer
VIRGIL
The Aeneid
ALICE WALKER
The Color Purple
KEITH WATERHOUSE
Billy Liar
EVELYN WAUGH
Decline and Fall
JOHN WEBSTER
The Duchess of Malfi
OSCAR WILDE
The Importance of Being Earnest
THORNTON WILDER
Our Town
TENNESSEE WILLIAMS
The Glass Menagerie
VIRGINIA WOOLF
Mrs Dalloway
To the Lighthouse
WILLIAM WORDSWORTH
Selected Poems
WILLIAM WYCHERLEY
The Country Wife
W. B. YEATS
Selected Poems